Roots

vocabulary for life

Volume 1

L. Phipps

Visit **rootsvocab.com** for corresponding online activities and assessments.

*Dedicated to my wonderful students, past, present, and future,
and to all who keep love of language alive.*

With deep thanks to the Friends Seminary Sabbatical Committee (2015-2016), Bo Lauder, Leitzel Schoen, Maria Fahey, Craig Saslow, Lauren Anderson, Pankti Sevak, Rachelle Scolari, Justin Shearer, and Kieryn Phipps.

*Copyright © 2017 by L. Phipps. All rights reserved.
This publication, or any part thereof, may not be reproduced in any form,
or by any means, without the written permission of the author.
Address inquiries to: info@rootsvocab.com*

Table of Contents

What Is Roots?
Important Concepts
Introduction 1: The English Language 1
Introduction 2: Parts of Speech, Suffixes, and Prefixes 6
Introduction 3: How Each Lesson Works 11
Lesson 1: Not 13
in/im, il/ir, non, un, dis
Lesson 2: With, Without, Between, Around 21
co/col, con/com, a/an, inter, circ
Lesson 3: Backwards, Before, After 29
retro, pre, ante/antiq, fore, post
Lesson 4: Back, For, Against 37
re, pro, ant/anti, contra, ob/op
Lesson 5: Both, Many, All 45
ambi, multi, poly, omni, pan
Lesson 6: More, Less, Half 53
super/sur, hyper, sub, hypo, semi
Lesson 7: Out, Away 61
ex/extr, e/ec, de, se, ab
Lesson 8: In, Across, Through 69
in/im, intro/intra, en/em, trans, per
Lesson 9: Same and Different 77
syn/sym, homo, equ, hetero, altr/alter
Lesson 10: Good, Right, True 85
ben/bene, bon, eu, rect, ver
Lesson 11: Bad, Wrong, False 93
dys, mal, err, mis, fall/fals
Lesson 12: Hear, See, Feel 101
audi, spect, vis, sens/sent, tact/tang
Lesson 13: One, Two 109
uni, mono, sol, bi, di/du
Lesson 14: Forces 117
pel/puls, ject, ten/tain, pend, tract
Notes

What is *Roots*?
Is this just another vocab workbook?

Like all vocabulary programs, *Roots* is about learning useful, high-level words. In this book, you will meet 120 words, and you will practice them in a variety of ways. But *Roots* is about more than just learning new words.

It's about what words are made of and how they work.

Beyond words, you will learn **roots, prefixes,** and **suffixes** – short fragments of meaning that are not words themselves but that can be found in most English words. When you learn a word part, you gain insight into the meaning of the many words that contain it. In fact, mastering just the 90 common roots, prefixes, and suffixes in this book will open up your access to *thousands* of words.

It's about mastering vocabulary for life, not just for school.

Roots is designed to activate your long-term memory. The goal is not just to pass assessments but to actually boost your working vocabulary so you can understand more and express yourself better, now and in the future. Roots is *cumulative*, which means all the words and roots you learn will reappear again and again throughout the program. Because you will keep encountering the words, you will have little opportunity to forget them. And you won't just memorize definitions – you'll actively *think* about words and work with them in a carefully sequenced series of activities, both in this book and online. By the end of this book, you will know many new words and word parts. Just as important, you will know how to use your new knowledge to find meaning in unfamiliar words you encounter.

Through Roots, you will:
- ❖ **master new words, word roots, prefixes, and suffixes**
- ❖ *practice in a way that helps you remember for the long haul*
- ❖ *learn how to make sense of unfamiliar words you come across*
- ❖ *strengthen your ability to think and reason*

And you may even have fun in the process! Oh – and just so you know, in *Roots*, *you* will NOT:
- ♦ memorize a long list of words, only to never see them again after the quiz
- ♦ spend hours studying flashcards (unless you want to)

Important Concepts

Before you begin, you should be familiar with a few basic terms and concepts.
- *If you already know these concepts, use this page to review.*
- *If these concepts are new to you, take time to learn them now.*
- *Turn back to this page whenever you need a reminder.*

word root	a word part that has meaning but cannot stand on its own *Example:* **vis** = see vi<u>vis</u>ual, re<u>vis</u>e, in<u>vis</u>ible, <u>vis</u>or, super<u>vis</u>e *Many English word roots have Latin and Greek origins.*
prefix	a letter or cluster of letters that, when put at the ***beginning*** of a word, changes its meaning *Examples:* <u>un</u>happy, <u>re</u>heat, <u>mis</u>spell, <u>dis</u>appear *Many English prefixes derive from Latin and Greek.*
suffix	a letter or cluster of letters that, when added to the ***end*** of a word, changes its part of speech or its meaning (slightly) *Examples:* thought → thought<u>ful</u> / approach → approach<u>able</u>
synonym	a word with the same or nearly the same meaning *Gigantic* is a synonym for *enormous*.
antonym	a word with the opposite or nearly opposite meaning *Beautiful* is an antonym for *ugly*.
homophone	a word that sounds the same but has a different meaning *See* and *sea* are homophones.
analogy	a comparison that shows how one pair of words is like another pair of words • **Eyes** are to **see** as **ears** are to **hear**. • **Happy** is to **sad** as **old** is to **young**.

Roots Volume 1   The English Language

Introduction 1: The English Language

> To understand why English has so many roots and prefixes,
> you first need to understand its place among languages.

Language Families

There are more than 7,000 distinct languages in the world, most of which can be grouped into 15 major language families. **A language family is a group of languages that share a common ancestor.** There are also a few rare languages that don't belong to any group; these are called *language isolates*. Language isolates are fascinating and worthy of your time and attention, but we will not discuss them further in this book because English is far from a language isolate: **English is part of the largest language family, Indo-European.** Almost three billion people speak Indo-European languages today. Below are the four largest language families and some of their languages.

Indo-European India, Europe, Middle East	*Afro-Asiatic* Middle East, Africa	*Sino-Tibetan* Asia	*Niger-Congo* Africa
~	~	~	~
Hindi	Arabic	Mandarin Chinese	Yoruba
Greek	Hebrew	Cantonese	Swahili
Russian	Hausa	Burmese	Igbo
Spanish	Amharic	Tibetan	Fula
English	Turkish	Karenic	Shona
etc.	etc.	etc.	etc.

Within language families, languages can be very different from each other. Russian and Spanish, for example, are both Indo-European languages, but you certainly cannot understand one if you only speak the other. **Being in the same language family does not mean being the same language** -- it just means sharing a common origin.

To remember: *English is in the Indo-European language family.*

Roots Volume 1 — The English Language

Indo-European
our big language family

Within major language families, there are smaller language families, and these can often be further divided into smaller groups again and again until you get down to each individual language. The **Indo-European language family has many subgroups**, the largest of which are listed in the chart below with some of their languages.

Germanic Western and Northern Europe	*Romance* Western and Southern Europe	*Balto-Slavic* Eastern Europe	*Indo-Iranian* India and the Middle East
German	Italian	Russian	Hindi
Swedish	French	Czech	Bengali
Dutch	Spanish	Bulgarian	Farsi
Danish	Portuguese	Polish	Urdu
English	Romanian	Serbo-Croatian	Marathi

Germanic
our smaller language family

As you can see above, **English is a Germanic language**. The Anglo-Saxons who settled in England beginning around 400 A.D. came from Germanic-speaking areas in Western Europe and spoke several languages that eventually blended together and became English. Though there were other languages spoken in England at the time, it was English that quickly became dominant. The word *English*, in fact, comes from the name of one of the settling tribes, the Angles. English has changed significantly over the years, but modern English still has a lot in common with its Germanic language cousins. Look at the following words:

English	Dutch	Swedish	German
book	boek	bok	Buch
cow	koe	ko	Kuh
house	huis	hus	Haus
hand	hand	hand	Hand

To remember: **English is a Germanic language.**

Roots Volume 1   The English Language

Our Latin and Greek Roots

Latin was the language of ancient Rome, heavily influenced by ancient Greek. While it is now extinct as a living language, several modern languages developed from it, including French (see Romance languages, p. 2). Germanic languages do *not* derive from Latin, and as you know, English is a Germanic language. Yet, in modern English **more than 60 percent of words have Latin or Greek origins.** That's right: English is a Germanic language, but the majority of its words are *not* Germanic. What? Why? How? The answer goes back to England's complicated history.

Anglo-Saxons Arrive

400 A.D. – 500 A.D. -- Anglo-Saxon tribes from Denmark and other Germanic areas began settling in Britain. Each tribe had its own language, but the languages were similar enough that they soon merged into one language: English.

Christianity Arrives

500 A.D. to 700 A.D. – Christianity was introduced to England on a large scale shortly after the Anglo-Saxons settled. In 601 A.D., the first Christian Anglo-Saxon king was crowned, and by 700 A.D., almost everyone in England was Christian. The Church was ruled from Rome (Italy) by a pope and was, in many ways, more influential and powerful than the king. Since **Latin was the official language of the Church**, those in England who wanted influence and power made sure to learn it. Some Latin-based words entered English during this period.

A French-Speaking King Arrives (and Conquers!)

1066 A.D. to 1399 A.D. – In 1066 A.D., William the Conqueror and his large army invaded England. He was a French speaker from Normandy (northern France), and after he won the fight and claimed the throne, he gave away much of England's land to his friends, French nobles. They brought their language with them. Over the next few hundred years, Latin remained the language of the Church, and **French became the language of royalty**, nobility, judges, and scholars. Now, anyone in England who wanted power and influence learned French as well as Latin. As more English people learned French, more French words entered English. (Remember, French is derived from Latin, which is heavily influenced by Greek.)

To remember: *Words derived from Latin and Greek entered English through French, which was once the language of royalty and nobility in England. Latin was also the language of the very powerful Church.*

English: A Language of Synonyms
Cow vs. Beef

While French and Latin were the languages of power, English remained the language of the people. The simple farmers, laborers, and craftspeople who made up the majority of the population never learned French or Latin. By the time last French-speaking king died in 1413 A.D., French and Latin had become so widespread among the powerful that they continued to study them for generations afterward, but even the wealthiest and most educated people usually spoke English at home. That means French words did not replace English words but became additional words, increasing our vocabulary and giving us so many synonyms. We often have two words for the same thing because we still have the original Germanic word *and* the borrowed French/Latin/Greek word. The borrowed words tend to be higher-level words because they were once used only by the wealthiest and most educated citizens.

Consider the words *beef* and *cow*. Both refer to the same animal, but one refers to the form of the animal you can eat, and the other just to the animal itself. Ordinary English people rarely ate cow meat because they could not afford it. The wealthy, however, could afford cow meat, which in French was called *boeuf*. These wealthy English, borrowing from French, began to call the food on their plates *beef* to distinguish it from the animals in the field. And thus, a synonym pair was born. It's the same story with *chicken* vs. *poultry*, *sheep* vs. *mutton*, and many other synonyms. Take a look at some more synonym pairs, and notice how the borrowed words seem more advanced than the Germanic words.

Original English (Germanic)	Borrowed from French
graveyard	cemetery
brotherly	fraternal
same	equivalent
rich	affluent
green	verdant
sight	vision
sadness	melancholy

In modern English, you can be a *book-lover* (Germanic) or a *bibliophile* (borrowed). You can *do well* (Germanic) or you can *succeed* (borrowed). You can be *friendly* (Germanic) or you can be *amiable* (borrowed). And now you know why!

Roots Volume 1 — The English Language

Modern English
The Latin/Greek Influence Remains

As Britain began to colonize many areas of the world in the 17th through 19th centuries, the English language spread far and wide. North America, Europe, Africa, and Australia all have large numbers of native English speakers, and English is a second language for billions of people across the world.

To remember: *English is the most widely-spoken language in the world.*

English has continued to borrow words from other languages, and our vocabulary is now peppered with words from all over, such as *alligator* (from Spanish), *bandana* (from Hindi), and *squash* (from Narragansett, a Native American language). Nevertheless, **the greatest outside influence on English has come from Latin/Greek.** More than 60 percent of all our words have Latin/Greek origins. And in the fields of science and technology, more than 90 percent do.

To remember: *More than 60 percent of English words have Latin/Greek roots or prefixes, including more than 90 percent of scientific and technical terms.*

By now, you can see for yourself why **understanding Latin/Greek roots and prefixes is an important key to understanding English**. As you read more advanced texts, your knowledge of word roots will help you decipher the many high-level words that derive from Latin and Greek. These are the kind of words that people often call "tricky," but when you know many roots and prefixes, they become more like puzzles waiting to be pieced together. For example, once you know that **sub** is a prefix meaning "below" and **terr** is a root meaning "earth," you can make sense of a word like **subterranean**, which means "below the earth; underground."

By the end of this book, you will see words differently. You will have important clues as to what many advanced words mean. You will have a sense of where they came from and why they exist. You will have a richer understanding of your own language.

> Learning about language families and language history can be fascinating. The study of human language is called **linguistics**, and it is a broad and exciting field. If your curiosity has been piqued, start exploring!

Learn more about language families and English language history at rootsvocab.com.

Introduction 2: Parts of Speech, Suffixes, and Prefixes

> Have you learned about the **parts of speech** before? If so, this lesson is a good review. If not, don't worry – the main ideas are easy to understand.

The Parts of Speech

There are eight kinds of words, called the **parts of speech:**
nouns, pronouns, verbs, adjectives, adverbs, prepositions, conjunctions, interjections.
The vast majority of words fit into only the four main categories below.

noun	adjective	verb	adverb
person, place, thing, idea	describes a noun – tells "what kind"	action word (something you can <u>do</u>)	describes how a verb is done

NOUNS
people, places, things, ideas

People	Places	Things	Ideas
teacher	Chicago	pencil	anger
Adam	forest	oxygen	Tuesday
toddler	village	Oreo	The Civil War

Many high-level nouns in English are **ideas**. An idea is a "thing" that is abstract or does not have a physical existence (e.g., *trust, month, July, freedom, sadness, century, brilliance, admiration, The Great Depression, excitement, winter, civility, democracy*).

Many of the nouns you will learn in this book denote <u>ideas</u>.

Roots Volume 1 — Parts of Speech, Suffixes, and Prefixes

ADJECTIVES describe people, places, things, and ideas *which? how many? whose?*	VERBS are physical or mental actions; things that *can happen* or that *can be done*	ADVERBS tell more about a verb, adjective, or other adverb *how? how often? when? where? to what extent?*
pleasant	*jump*	*quietly*
those	*sleep*	*unremarkably*
twenty	*decide*	*yesterday*
your	*imagine*	*very*

Knowing a word's part of speech helps you figure out what the word means and how to use it when you speak and write.

Suffixes

You can often tell a word's part of speech by looking at its **suffix**, or ending. A suffix is a letter or letter cluster that has no meaning by itself but that slightly changes the meaning of the base word to which it is added. A suffix is always at the <u>end</u> of a word. Here are a few basic examples:

dog	→	dog**s**	farm	→	farm**er**
warm	→	warm**er**	know	→	know**n**
tall	→	tall**est**	mistake	→	mistak**en**
go	→	go**ing**	sun	→	sun**y**
jump	→	jump**ed**	style	→	styl**ish**

Notice that the *part of speech* of a word can change when a suffix is added. For example, **mistake, sun,** and **style** are nouns. Add suffixes and they become adjectives: **mistak<u>en</u>, sunn<u>y</u>,** and **styl<u>ish</u>.** When you learn which part of speech a suffix usually denotes (suggests), you get an important hint about words that end with that suffix.

❖ **Example:** A word that ends with –*ish* is almost always going to be an adjective. If you see the word *fiendish*, you can tell that it's probably an adjective, even if you don't know what it means. The suffix tells you that it's likely a word used to describe a person, place, thing, or idea.

Look at the way a single word's meaning and part of speech can change depending upon the suffix:

excite → excite**s** → excite**d** → excit**ing** → excit**able** → excite**ment** → excited**ly**

Prefixes

While suffixes come at the end of words, **prefixes** are letters or letter clusters that come at the beginning of words and add some kind of meaning.

<mark>heat → **re**heat   kind → **un**kind   appear → **dis**appear   migrate → **im**migrate</mark>

Like suffixes, they can help you make sense of new words. Unlike suffixes, however, prefixes <u>do not</u> change a word's part of speech. You will meet many prefixes in *Roots*.

To Remember

1. There are eight parts of speech, but most words can be categorized as either nouns, verbs, adjectives, or adverbs.

2. A **prefix** is a letter or letter cluster that comes at the <u>beginning</u> of a word and adds meaning. Prefixes do not change the part of speech.
    Example: **happy → <u>un</u>happy**

3. A **suffix** is a letter or letter cluster that comes at the <u>end</u> of word and often changes its part of speech.
    Example: **fame → fam<u>ous</u>**

4. Identifying a word's prefix can give you clues as to its meaning. Identifying a word's suffix can help you figure out a word's part of speech. Both can help you make sense of the word so that you can better make sense of what you are reading.

> *Whenever you encounter a new word in a text,*
> *see whether there is a suffix, prefix, and/or word root you recognize.*
> *You may get an important clue that will help you make sense of the word.*

Roots Volume 1 — Parts of Speech, Suffixes, and Prefixes

Common Suffixes

As you encounter new words, you will see certain suffixes again and again. These are worth learning. Below are some of the most common suffixes, many of which you will observe as you work through *Roots*. Though there are some exceptions, the great majority of the time these suffixes suggest the parts of speech indicated below.

Noun Suffix	Example	Your Examples (write one or two each)
-ness	softness	
-ity	creativity	
-tion, -sion	attention, vision	
-ment	achievement	
-ance, -ence	distance, sequence	
-ancy, -ency	vacancy, frequency	
-ism	magnetism	
-tude	altitude	
-cian, -tian	magician, Christian	

Adjective Suffix	Example	Your Examples (write one or two each)
-al, -ial	magical, financial	
-ic	scientific	
-ive	attentive	
-ent	persistent	
-able, -ible	traceable, visible	
-less	hopeless	
-ful	joyful	
-ous	anonymous	

Verb Suffix	Example	Your Examples (write one or two each)
-ize	realize	
-fy	identify	

Adverb Suffix	Example	Your Examples (write one or two each)
-ly	noisily	

Roots Volume 1 — Parts of Speech, Suffixes, and Prefixes

> **PRACTICE: Can you infer a word's part of speech?**
> For each word, circle the suffix and write which part of speech it suggests.
> You can abbreviate: **N** (noun), **ADJ** (adjective), **V** (verb), **and ADV** (adverb)

1. parlance _____

2. festive _____

3. fortitude _____

4. fraternize _____

5. baleful _____

6. practical _____

7. personable _____

8. plausible _____

9. dutifully _____

10. raucous _____

11. evident _____

12. rustic _____

13. deify _____

14. feudalism _____

15. consternation _____

16. civility _____

Practice identifying suffixes at rootsvocab.com.

Introduction 3: How Each Lesson Works

❖ *In each lesson, you will meet **5 roots/prefixes** and **10 words**.*
❖ *All lessons follow the same sequence of exercises, divided into eight steps.*
❖ *It is important to **complete the lessons and steps in order** and to spread the steps out over at least a few days.* Roots *is not as effective if you cram, so please don't try to complete an entire lesson in one day!*

STEP 1: Examine the Words
How well do you know them? What can you tell about them?

Look at each word closely. How well do you know it? While many words will be new, some words may already be familiar to you. This is just fine. Remember, your goal is to *master* the words, not merely to know them, so practicing familiar words can be just as valuable as learning new ones.

STEP 2: Figure Out Meaning
Using context and your knowledge of roots, write the <u>sentence number</u> of the bolded word next to the best definition below. *Note: Not all definitions will be used.*

Your next step is to try to figure out the meaning of each word by thinking about its root or prefix and then looking at the way it is used in a sentence. Inferring meanings for yourself is great mental exercise and an important step in helping you remember what you are learning.

STEP 3: Use the Words in Sentences
For each sentence on the next page, fill in the word from the list that <u>best</u> fits the blank. *Note: Words may be used twice.*

Once you have had a try at figuring meanings out for yourself, turn to a list of words with their definitions, parts of speech, and derivatives (other forms of the word). Use the list and your own powers of logic to figure out which word best fits in each blank in a list of sentences.

Roots Volume 1 How Each Lesson Works

STEP 4: Review What You Know
How much do you remember? Let's find out!

This is a varied review of previously learned words, roots, and prefixes. You will notice that each question in Step 4 is in a different font. This is on purpose! Seeing words in different fonts has been shown to help people remember them better later. It's also a little weird, which makes it a little interesting, which makes it a little more fun.

STEP 5: Write the Words
Write each word one more time (in any order). Be sure to spell correctly!

When your brain makes hand-mind connections, it can help plant the words in your long-term memory. It also, of course, helps with spelling.

STEP 6: Dig a Little Deeper
Deepen and express your understanding in different ways.

Make your own sentences, figure out the meanings of new words based on your knowledge of familiar ones, draw pictures or symbols to represent words, and complete other open-ended exercises. Each lesson has a different set of exercises.

STEP 7: Examine Other Words
Check any words you already know well.
Put an **X** next to words you do not know well or do not know at all.

Take a look at other words with the same roots and prefixes you have just learned. Which do you already know, and which are new to you?

STEP 8: Reflect on the Meaning of New Words
Choose two of the words that you do not already know and look up their meanings.
Consider how the *root* in each word relates to its meaning.

Sometimes, the way a root or prefix relates to a word's meaning is obvious. Other times, you may have to dig deeper into the origins of a word to see how the root or prefix influences meaning. **Google dictionary**, **Dictionary.com** and **The Oxford Living Dictionary** are online resources that provide word origins for every entry.

Practice activities and assessments for all lessons can be found at rootvocab.com.

Roots Volume 1

Lesson 1: Not

in/im	il/ir	non	un	dis
not	not	not	not	not; away

incompetence unwitting illogical disparage nondescript
dispel uncouth impartial nonentity irrelevant

STEP 1: Examine and Categorize the Words
How well do you know them? What can you tell about them?

New Words	Familiar Words	Known Words	Mastered Words
words I do not know; unfamiliar words	words I recognize but cannot fully define	words I understand but don't use often	words I know well and use regularly

1. **Impartial** and **illogical** share the same suffix. Circle it.
   What part of speech does it suggest? _____

2. What is the suffix of the word **nonentity**? Circle it.
   What part of speech does it suggest? _____

3. What is the suffix of the word **incompetence**? Circle it.
   What part of speech does it suggest? _____

Need help remembering the suffixes? Turn back to p. 9.

Roots Volume 1 — Lesson 1

> **STEP 2: Figure Out Meaning**
> Using context and your knowledge of roots, write the <u>sentence number</u> of the bolded word next to the best definition below. *Note: Not all definitions will be used.*

1. After three days of burned meats, overly salty soups, and flavorless side dishes, the new chef was fired for **incompetence.**

2. As long as the machine works, it is **irrelevant** to me how you build it.

3. I know I failed the test, but please do not **disparage** my efforts. I really did try.

4. Hoping to **dispel** his friend's anger, Anthony wrote a heartfelt apology note.

5. In his **nondescript** outfit of jeans and a T-shirt, Jim blended right in with the crowd.

6. Not a single person said hello to her or even smiled, causing Lily to feel like a **nonentity.**

7. It is **illogical** to expect people to trust you if you have a history of lying.

8. We trusted the referee because we knew he was **impartial.**

9. The **unwitting** gentleman hummed a cheerful tune as the thief picked his pocket.

10. We were shocked by the shopkeeper's rude language and **uncouth** behavior.

fair; not favoring one side over another	not important; not related	dull and ordinary; not interesting or distinctive	not having good or proper manners	to make go away (a feeling or idea)	not reasonable; not making sense
not appreciative; ungrateful	nonexistent or unimportant thing/person	not knowing; not aware	not having a sense of humor	not having the ability to do a job well	to speak badly of; to put down (verbally)

Roots Volume 1 — Lesson 1

> **STEP 3: Use Words in Sentences**
> For each sentence on the next page, fill in the word from the list that <u>best</u> fits the blank. *Note: Words may be used twice.*

IN/IM not	**incompetence** (n) *incompetent (adj)*	**not** having the ability to do a job successfully
	impartial (adj) *impartiality (n)*	fair; **not** favoring one side over another
IL/IR not	**illogical** (adj) *illogically (adv)*	**not** reasonable; **not** making sense
	irrelevant (adj) *irrelevance (n)*	**not** important in the current context; **not** related to the current situation or context
NON not	**nondescript** (adj)	**not** interesting or distinctive; dull and ordinary
	nonentity (n)	a person or thing that is **not** important or that does **not** exist; a "nobody"
UN not	**uncouth** (adj)	**not** having good or proper manners or behavior
	unwitting (adj) *unwittingly (adv)*	**not** knowing; **not** aware
DIS not; away	**dispel** (v)	to make go **away** (a feeling or idea)
	disparage (v) *disparaging (adj)*	to speak badly of; to put down (verbally); *lit. to suggest that something or someone is **not** at a high level

---

* *Lit.* means *literally* and refers to the actual meaning of a word, which is sometimes slightly different from how it is commonly used.

Roots Volume 1   Lesson 1

1. Sara tried to remain _____, but in the end, she couldn't help but favor her brother.

2. Though he was raggedy and _____, Fiona believed she could teach Delroy to become a proper gentleman.

3. Maria was a(n) _____ bystander, clueless about what was happening around her.

4. The king was furious when the prince chose as his wife a(n) _____ -- a poor farm girl from a small village.

5. Everyone was surprised when Katherine, despite her _____, was promoted to a higher position within the company.

6. Detective Anders waded through pages of interesting but _____ information before coming across something that might help her solve the case.

7. Making an umbrella out of tissue paper is completely _____.

8. Only the plane's pilots knew how close they had come to collision; the _____ passengers remained calm and content.

9. The museum housed a _____ collection of paintings, and we soon grew bored.

10. I hope the new security system will _____ any fears visitors have about staying safe in our hotel.

11. Say what you will about lazy Thomas, but do not _____ his hard-working family.

12. Though a kind man, Alan was remembered best for his _____; in his five years on the detective force, he had never solved a single crime.

13. To be a good judge, you must be _____ and consider only the evidence presented.

14. Nutritionists try to _____ the myth that your diet has no effect on your health.

16

Roots Volume 1

Lesson 1

> **STEP 4: Review What You Know**
> How much do you remember? Let's find out!

1. Which of the following might describe a good judge or referee?
   a. uncouth
   b. unwitting
   c. impartial
   d. incompetent

2. Why might someone choose to wear **nondescript** clothing?
   a. to blend in with others
   b. to be admired
   c. to be noticed
   d. to stay warm

3. *Uncouth* is to *polite* as **difficult** is to:
   a. impossible
   b. possible
   c. challenging
   d. easy

4. Which of the following is an antonym for **unwitting**?
   a. friendly
   b. aware
   c. polite
   d. fair

5. English is a(n) _____ language?
   A. Romance
   B. Afro-Asiatic
   C. Germanic
   D. French

6. Which suffix does NOT suggest that a word is an **adjective**?
   a. –ity
   b. –al
   c. –ful
   d. –ous

7. Which suffix(es) suggests that a word is an **adverb**?
   a. –tion, –sion
   b. –less
   c. –ence, –ency
   d. –ly

8. Which word below is NOT a noun?
   a. fish
   b. freedom
   c. frisbee
   d. frighten

9. Which is NOT a reason that English has so many Latin/Greek root words?
   a. French words (with Latin/Greek roots) were introduced during and after the Norman invasion of England in 1066 A.D.
   b. During the Middle Ages in England, French (with Latin/Greek roots) was the language of the courts, the nobility, and the universities.
   c. For hundreds of years, Latin was the language of the Church in England.
   d. English is a Romance language, like French and Spanish.

Roots Volume 1　　　　　　　　　　　　　　　　　　　　Lesson 1

10. If a word ends with the suffix *-able* or *-ible*, it is likely to be a(n):
    a. noun
    b. verb
    c. adjective
    d. adverb

11. If you want to **dispel** an idea, you might:
    a. tell people about the idea
    b. adopt the idea
    c. prove the idea is wrong
    d. support the idea with evidence

12. Look at the suffix. **Resolute*ness*** is a(n):
    a. noun
    b. verb
    c. adjective
    d. adverb

13. If you overhear someone saying **disparaging** things about you, you might feel:
    a. happy
    b. sad or angry
    c. tired
    d. excited

14. Which of the following would be an *irrelevant* detail in an essay about Abraham Lincoln's life?
    a. when Lincoln was born
    b. how Lincoln became president
    c. what Lincoln accomplished as president
    d. how many Americans have the last name Lincoln

15. **Impatient** and **impartial**:
    a. are synonyms
    b. are antonyms
    c. have the same prefix
    d. have the same suffix

16. **Celebrity** is to *unknown* as **nonentity** is to:
    a. important
    b. lonely
    c. wild
    d. unimportant

17. Look at the suffix. **Euphem*ism*** is a(n):
    a. adverb
    b. verb
    c. adjective
    d. noun

18. One way a prefix differs from a suffix is that a **prefix**:
    a. comes at the beginning of a word
    b. changes a word's part of speech
    c. is uncommon
    d. does not change a word's meaning

Roots Volume 1

Lesson 1

> **STEP 5: Write the Words**
> Write each word one more time (in any order). Be sure to spell correctly!

> incompetence   unwitting   illogical   disparage   nondescript
> dispel   uncouth   impartial   nonentity   irrelevant

_____   _____

_____   _____

_____   _____

_____   _____

> **STEP 6: Dig a Little Deeper**
> Deepen and express your understanding in different ways.

1. From your understanding of the prefix *in* and the word *incompetence*, what can you infer that **competence** means? Write a definition below.

2. Make up a sentence that correctly includes <u>two</u> words from the list. If you can't think of one single sentence, write two related sentences.

3. Choose one word from the list (any word): _____
   Draw a picture below to symbolize it or show what it means:

Roots Volume 1

Lesson 1

> **STEP 7: Examine Other Words**
> Check any words you already know well.
> Put an **X** next to words you do not know well or do not know at all.

IN/IM	IL/IR	NON
☐ inconsiderate	☐ illegal	☐ nonessential
☐ innocent	☐ illiterate	☐ nonchalant
☐ inconceivable	☐ illegitimate	☐ nonplussed
☐ impossible	☐ irregular	☐ nonverbal
☐ imprecise	☐ irresponsible	☐ nonsense
☐ immobile	☐ irreversible	

UN	DIS
☐ unpopular	☐ disease
☐ unknown	☐ dismay
☐ unnoticed	☐ disappear
☐ unabridged	☐ disjointed
☐ unbelievable	☐ dispirited
☐ unappreciated	☐ disenfranchise

> **STEP 8: Reflect on the Meaning of New Words**
> Choose two of the words that you do <u>not</u> already know and look up their meanings. Consider how the **root** in each word relates to its meaning.

Word: Word:

Meaning: Meaning:

in/im	il/ir	non	un	dis
not	not	not	not	not; away

Roots Volume 1   Lesson 2

Lesson 2: With, Without, Between, Around

co/col	con/com	a/an	inter	circ
with	with	without	between	around

coherent   colleague   concur   compatible   abyss
apathy   intercede   interim   circuitous   circumvent

STEP 1: Examine the Words
How well do you know them? What can you tell about them?

New Words	Familiar Words	Known Words	Mastered Words
words I do not know; unfamiliar words	words I recognize but cannot fully define	words I understand but don't use often	words I know well and use regularly

1. What is the suffix of the word **circuitous**? Circle it.
   What part of speech does it suggest?   _____

2. **Co/col** is a SYNONYM for which other prefix from this lesson?   _____

3. **Co/col** is an ANTONYM for which other prefix from this lesson?   _____

4. What is the suffix of the word **compatible**? Circle it.
   What part of speech does it suggest?   _____

Need help remembering the suffixes? Turn back to p. 9.

Roots Volume 1 — Lesson 2

> **STEP 2: Figure Out Meaning**
> Using context and your knowledge of roots, write the underlined sentence number of the bolded word next to the best definition below. *Note: Not all definitions will be used.*

1. I was shocked by his **apathy** in the face of danger. Even though he could have been killed, he expressed no fear, alarm, anger, or surprise.

2. Because his essay was **coherent** and well written, we had no trouble understanding his ideas.

3. The two friends were perfectly **compatible** and never annoyed each other.

4. We have now all heard Charlie's opinion. If you **concur** with it, raise your hand.

5. Though the pit couldn't have been more than a few feet deep, it seemed like an **abyss** to poor, frightened Henry.

6. If things get difficult at work, ask a supportive **colleague** for advice.

7. There's an hour between dinner and the movie. In the **interim**, get some rest.

8. We tried to **circumvent** the tall mountain, but in the end, we had to climb it.

9. If the twins start fighting again, will you please **intercede**?

10. He gave me a long, **circuitous** answer when all I wanted was a "yes" or "no."

able to get along well or go together	person with whom one works	deep or bottomless hole	going around; not straight or direct	clear and understandable	angry and bitter; overly jealous
being lazy; avoiding hard work	state of not caring; lack of feeling or concern	to get around (a problem or obstacle)	to agree (with someone or something)	to come between people in conflict	the time in between; temporary

Roots Volume 1 — Lesson 2

> **STEP 3: Use Words in Sentences**
> For each sentence on the next page, fill in the word from the list that <u>best</u> fits the blank. *Note: Words may be used twice.*

CO/COL with; together	**coherent** (adj) *coherence (n)* *coherently (adv)*	clear and understandable; making sense; *lit. sticking* **together**
	colleague (n)	person **with** whom one works professionally
CON/COM with; together	**concur** (v) *concurrence (n)* *concurrently (adv)*	to agree **with** (someone or something); to happen **together** (at the same time)
	compatible (adj) *compatibility (n)*	able to get along without conflict; able to go **together**
A/AN without	**abyss** (n)	deep hole or chasm; endless pit (*lit.* "**without** bottom"); intense unpleasant mental state
	apathy (n) *apathetic (adj)*	the state of being **without** emotional response (not feeling or caring)
INTER between	**intercede** (v) *intercession (n)*	to come **between** others in order to solve a problem or resolve conflict
	interim (n, adj)	the time **between** (n); only for a while; temporary (adj)
CIRC around	**circuitous** (adj)	going **around**; not direct or straightforward
	circumvent (v)	to go **around** (a problem or obstacle)

Roots Volume 1   Lesson 2

1. The play ended at four and dinner was at six. In the _____, we played cards on the lawn.

2. The straight road will get you there more quickly, but the _____ trail offers better views.

3. Though I should have been thrilled at winning the game, all I experienced was _____.

4. Michael feels we should go home early. Do you _____?

5. As they walked through the portal, the ground gave way and they fell headlong into a dark _____.

6. If you don't _____ and help bring an end to their feud, I'm afraid they might never speak to each other again.

7. After seven years in the office together, Laura considered Margaret to be not just a(n) _____ but also a friend.

8. The burglar found a clever way to _____ the alarm system.

9. If your speech is not _____, it will be hard to understand.

10. Is this software program _____ with your old computer?

11. If we cannot _____ this problem, we will not make any further progress.

12. After arguing every day for three months, the roommates decided they were simply not _____.

13. Researchers are trying to find ways to overcome voter _____ and get more citizens to care about the upcoming election.

14. When her dog died, Anna fell into a(n) _____ of sadness.

15. As I read his brilliant plan, I couldn't help but nod my head and _____ on every point.

Roots Volume 1

Lesson 2

> **STEP 4: Review What You Know**
> How much do you remember? Let's find out!

1. **Uncouth** behavior might also be described as:
   a. rude and unrefined
   b. polite and respectful
   c. strange
   d. frightening

2. If you are experiencing **apathy**, you are not experiencing:
   a. being popular
   b. being polite
   c. being angry
   d. being safe

3. Because she lacked influence and fame, Alexa always felt like a(n) _____ in her community:
   a. colleague
   b. nonentity
   c. abyss
   d. interim

4. *Fettered* means "restricted; held back." **Unfettered** means:
   a. very restricted
   b. unhappy
   c. able to be restricted
   d. not restricted

5. Over ninety percent of scientific and technological terms in English have:
   a. Latin or Greek roots
   b. Russian roots
   c. Germanic roots
   d. Celtic roots

6. Which suffix(es) suggest(s) that a word is a NOUN?
   a. –tion, -sion
   b. –eous, -ious
   c. –ly
   d. –ive, -itive, -ative

7. To keep your essay _____, do not include a lot of _____ details.
   a. coherent . . . irrelevant
   b. illogical . . . unwitting
   c. uncouth . . . compatible
   d. impartial . . . apathetic

8. Which word below is NOT an adjective?
   a. cozy
   b. sadly
   c. tall
   d. delicate

9. If you want to **dispel** a feeling, you want to make it:
   a. become stronger
   b. spread widely
   c. change
   d. go away

Roots Volume 1   Lesson 2

10. If a word ends with the suffix *-fy* or *-ize*, it is likely to be a(n):
    a. noun
    b. verb
    c. adjective
    d. adverb

11. If you *disparage* someone, you:
    a. speak badly of them
    b. praise them
    c. get to know them
    d. befriend them

12. Based on your understanding of the word *impartial*, what does **partial** mean?
    a. taking one side over another
    b. never choosing sides
    c. fair and unbiased
    d. rational; making sense

13. *Legitimate* means "according to law." Something that is **illegitimate** is:
    a. sometimes according to law
    b. not according to law
    c. always according to law
    d. usually according to law

14. Based on your understanding of the word *coherent* and the root *in*, consider what *incoherent* likely means. Which word from Lesson 1 has a similar meaning?
    a. irrelevant
    b. illogical
    c. incompetent
    d. impartial

15. Which word below is an **abstract noun** (an idea)?
    a. friendly
    b. friend
    c. friendless
    d. friendship

16. Which is true about suffixes?
    a. They can come at the beginning or end of words.
    b. They never change the part of speech of a word.
    c. They can change the part of speech of a word.
    d. Every word must have one.

17. If something is **nondescript**, it is:
    a. uninteresting and ordinary
    b. exciting and new
    c. incapable of doing a job well
    d. unimportant or nonexistent

18. **Someone who demonstrates *incompetence* might not:**
    a. **be hired for an important job**
    b. **be aware of what is going on**
    c. **be fair and unbiased**
    d. **be polite and well-mannered**

19. English is part of which large language family?
    a. Indo-European
    b. Afro-Asiatic
    c. Sino-Tibetan
    d. none of the above

Roots Volume 1 — Lesson 2

> **STEP 5: Write the Words**
> Write each word one more time (in any order). Be sure to spell correctly!

> coherent   colleague   concur   compatible   abyss
> apathy   intercede   interim   circuitous   circumvent

_____   _____

_____   _____

_____   _____

_____   _____

_____   _____

> **STEP 6: Dig a Little Deeper**
> Deepen and express your understanding in different ways.

1. From your understanding of the root *ir* and the word *irrelevant*, what can you infer that **relevant** means? Write a definition below.

2. Make up a sentence that correctly includes <u>two</u> words from the list. If you can't think of one single sentence, write two related sentences.

3. Choose one word from the list (any word):_____
Draw a picture below to symbolize it or show what it means:

Roots Volume 1　　　　　　　　　　　　　　　　　　　　　　　Lesson 2

> **STEP 7: Examine Other Words**
> Check any words you already know well.
> Put an **X** next to words you do not know well or do not know at all.

CO/COL	CON/COM	A/AN
☐ coworker	☐ condone	☐ amoral
☐ coexist	☐ consternation	☐ apolitical
☐ collision	☐ congratulate	☐ atheist
☐ collude	☐ communicate	☐ anaerobic
	☐ committee	
	☐ commotion	

INTER	CIRC
☐ interrupt	☐ circuit
☐ interval	☐ circle
☐ intermediary	☐ circumnavigate
☐ interject	☐ circus
☐ intervene	
☐ interact	
☐ intermittent	

> **STEP 8: Reflect on the Meaning of New Words**
> Choose two of the words that you do not already know and look up their meanings. Consider how the *root* in each word relates to its meaning.

Word:　　　　　　　　　　　　　　　　　Word:

Meaning:　　　　　　　　　　　　　　　Meaning:

co/col	con/com	a/an	inter	circ
with	with	without	between	around

Roots Volume 1

Lesson 3

Lesson 3: Backwards, Before, After

retro	pre	ante/antiq	fore	post
backwards	before	before	before	after; behind

prevail posthumous prejudice antiquated posterity
retrogress forewarn retrospect foresight antecedent

STEP 1: Examine the Words
How well do you know them? What can you tell about them?

New Words *words I do not know; unfamiliar words*	Familiar Words *words I recognize but cannot fully define*	Known Words *words I understand but don't use often*	Mastered Words *words I know well and use regularly*

1. What is the suffix of the word **posthumous**? Circle it.
   What part of speech does it suggest? _____

2. What is the suffix of the word **posterity**? Circle it.
   What part of speech does it suggest? _____

3. **PRE** and **POST** are:
   a. antonyms
   b. synonyms

29

Roots Volume 1 — Lesson 3

> **STEP 2: Figure Out Meaning**
> Using context and your knowledge of roots, write the <u>sentence number</u> of the bolded word next to the best definition below. *Note: Not all definitions will be used.*

1. Proud of her achievement after much hard work, Sophia declared she would never **retrogress** to being lazy and unmotivated.

2. Due to his **prejudice**, Tom assumed the neighbors were not his type of family before he got to know them.

3. Three months after her death, Kate received a **posthumous** achievement award.

4. Because he had **foresight**, Matthew packed a rain poncho for the long hike and was the only one of us who stayed dry when it started to pour.

5. I hated the swim class at the time, but in **retrospect**, I realize it was not so bad.

6. Think ahead into the future. What effect will your choices have on **posterity**?

7. The opponent appears weak, so I expect us to **prevail**.

8. Alice always loved the **antiquated** furniture and decorations at her grandma's house.

9. Getting a new job is often the **antecedent** to moving to a new home.

10. The old man tried to **forewarn** the children about the mysterious, dark cave.

strong; bold or adventurous	to go back to an earlier, worse state of being	looking back (to an earlier time)	judging before knowing	to lie; to cheat or acquire unfairly	happening after one's death
those who come after; future generations	what happens just before something else	to warn beforehand; to inform of possible danger	old-fashioned; from a time before	to win; to come before others	the ability to see or predict beforehand

Roots Volume 1 — Lesson 3

> **STEP 3: Use Words in Sentences**
> For each sentence on the next page, fill in the word from the list that best fits the blank. *Note: Words may be used twice.*

RETRO backwards	**retrogress** (v) *retrogression (n)*	to go **back** to an earlier, worse state of being
	retrospect (n) *retrospective (adj)*	state of looking **back** to an earlier time or thinking about the past
PRE before	**prejudice** (n) *prejudicial (adj)*	unfair judgment; judgment made **before** knowing the facts or the situation
	prevail (v) *prevailing (adj)*	to win or succeed; to come **before** others in a conflict or competition
ANTE/ ANTIQ before	**antecedent** (n)	event or situation that happens just **before** another event or situation (causing the second one to occur)
	antiquated (adj)	old-fashioned; out-of-date; from a time **before**
FORE before	**foresight** (n) *foresee (v)*	seeing **beforehand**; the ability to see (predict) in advance what might occur or be needed in the future
	forewarn (v)	to warn **before**hand; to inform of possible danger or difficulty
POST after; behind	**posthumous** (adj) *posthumously (adv)*	happening **after** one's death
	posterity (n)	the people to come **after**; future generations

Roots Volume 1 — Lesson 3

1. Go if you like, but I must _____ you that it will be a dangerous journey.

2. Though he realized he would likely never see the oak saplings grow to become trees, the old man planted them anyway for the sake of _____.

3. What was the _____ to her bizarre angry outburst? Did anyone see what happened?

4. Though as a child she had never known hunger, in _____, Dee realized that her family must have been quite poor.

5. If you don't replace these _____ computers with newer ones, you won't be able to use the new software.

6. The _____ release of the singer's final album comforted the many fans mourning her death.

7. Jill had the _____ to make more than enough food, so we all had plenty even though unexpected guests showed up.

8. We watched the match with great interest, eager to find out which team would _____.

9. With a heart free of _____, Kaylie gave everyone she met a fair chance to make a good impression.

10. We prayed that peace and love would _____ on earth.

11. Thank goodness Amelia had the _____ to board up the windows before the big storm hit!

12. When Spencer got out of prison, he vowed never to _____ to a life of crime.

13. His _____ style of dress made him look like he had stepped right out of an old movie.

14. In _____, I wish I had worried less and enjoyed myself more.

32

Roots Volume 1

Lesson 3

> **STEP 4: Mixed Review**
> How much do you remember? Let's find out!

1. *Mrs. Evans often shared teaching tips with **the other teachers at her school**.*
   a. her abysses
   b. her antecedents
   c. her colleagues
   d. her nonentities

2. Which is most likely to be described as an **abyss**?
   a. a dark hole or tunnel
   b. a poor farmer
   c. an impolite person
   d. an innocent child

3. Which of the following is likely to be a **verb**?
   a. marginalize
   b. vacuous
   c. conflagration
   d. itinerant

4. Which of the following is an ANTONYM for **concur**?
   a. emotional
   b. unclear
   c. challenge
   d. disagree

5. English belongs to which large language family?
   a. Sino-Tibetan
   b. Indo-European
   c. Afro-Asiatic
   d. Uralic

6. If you are unable to do your job successfully, you might be considered:
   a. nondescript
   b. compatible
   c. incompetent
   d. impartial

7. If you'd prefer the straightest, most direct route, then you <u>don't</u> want:
   a. the uncouth path
   b. the circuitous path
   c. the compatible path
   d. the retrospective path

8. IF YOU DON'T FEEL MUCH OF ANY KIND OF EMOTION, YOU ARE EXPERIENCING:
   A. POSTERITY
   B. APATHY
   C. RETROSPECT
   D. ANTECEDENT

9. If a word ends with the suffix *–tude* or *-tion*, it is likely to be a(n):
   a. noun
   b. verb
   c. adjective
   d. adverb

Roots Volume 1 — Lesson 3

10. If you *intercede* on behalf of someone, you
    a. come between that person and someone else
    b. speak badly of that person
    c. judge that person unfairly before knowing them
    d. get around that person

11. If a word ends with the suffix *-tude* or *-tion*, it is likely to be a(n):
    a. noun
    b. verb
    c. adjective
    d. adverb

12. Consider the meaning of *irrelevant*. What does *relevant* mean?
    a. related and important
    b. unrelated and unimportant
    c. getting along
    d. going around

13. Which is most likely to be considered **uncouth**?
    a. walking quickly
    b. singing beautifully
    c. eating sloppily
    d. laughing quietly

14. If you are **unwitting**, you are:
    a. alert and aware
    b. unknowing or unaware
    c. rude and inappropriate
    d. unimportant

15. Which can be ANTONYMS for **nondescript**?
    a. sad and lonely
    b. dull and ordinary
    c. secretive and mysterious
    d. unique and unusual

16. *Verbal* means "related to words." **Non-verbal** communication is:
    a. communication without words
    b. communication with words
    c. communication about words
    d. communication among people

17. A **cohesive** group of friends is a group that:
    a. sticks together
    b. bickers and argues
    c. breaks apart
    d. annoys others

18. If something exists in the *interim*, it exists:
    a. between two people
    b. only temporarily
    c. between places
    d. between things that go together

Roots Volume 1   Lesson 3

> **STEP 5: Write the Words**
> Write each word one more time (in any order). Be sure to spell correctly!

> prevail   posthumous   prejudice   antiquated   posterity
> retrogress   forewarn   retrospect   foresight   antecedent

_____   _____

_____   _____

_____   _____

_____   _____

> **STEP 6: Dig a Little Deeper**
> Deepen and express your understanding in different ways.

1. An **array** is an "ordered arrangement" of something. What might be found on the floor of a bedroom that has been left in **disarray**?

2. Make up a sentence that correctly includes <u>two</u> words from the list. If you can't think of one single sentence, write two related sentences.

3. Choose one word from the list (any word):_____
Draw a picture below to symbolize it or show what it means:

35

Roots Volume 1 — Lesson 3

> **STEP 7: Examine Other Words with the Same Prefix Roots**
> Check any words you already know well.
> Put an **X** next to words you do not know well or do not know at all.

RETRO	PRE	ANTE/ANTIQ
☐ retrograde	☐ preheat	☐ antediluvian
☐ retrofit	☐ precede	☐ antepasto
☐ retrofire	☐ precedent	☐ antique
☐ retrorocket	☐ preapprove	☐ antiquity
	☐ prevent	
	☐ presume	
	☐ predict	

FORE	POST
☐ foreground	☐ postmortem
☐ aforementioned	☐ posterior
☐ forethought	☐ postpone
☐ forehead	☐ postmodern
☐ foresee	☐ postwar
☐ forecast	
☐ unforeseen	
☐ foreshadow	

> **STEP 8: Reflect on the Meaning of New Words**
> Choose two of the words that you do not already know and look up their meanings. Consider how the **root** in each word relates to its meaning.

Word: Word:

Meaning: Meaning:

retro	pre	ante/antiq	fore	post
backwards	before	before	before	after; behind

Lesson 4: Back, For, Against

re	pro	ant/anti	contra	ob/op
back; again	for; forward	against	against	against

obstruct   contrary   propel   retaliate   profess
contradict   reticent   antidote   oppress   antagonist

STEP 1: Examine the Words
How well do you know them? What can you tell about them?

New Words	Familiar Words	Known Words	Mastered Words
words I do not know; unfamiliar words	words I recognize but cannot fully define	words I understand but don't use often	words I know well and use regularly

1. **Oppress*ive*** is what form of *oppress*? _____

2. **Retali*ation*** is what form of *retaliate*? _____

3. **Antagonist*ic*** is what form of *antagonist*? _____

4. PRO and ANTI are:
    a. antonyms
    b. synonyms

Roots Volume 1

Lesson 4

> **STEP 2: Figure Out Meaning**
> Using context and your knowledge of roots, write the <u>sentence number</u> of the bolded word next to the best definition below. *Note: Not all definitions will be used.*

1. **Contrary** to what we read on the website, the park entrance turned out to be closed.

2. While I talk about my problems openly, my brother is usually **reticent**.

3. The cruel king never lost an opportunity to **oppress** his subjects.

4. I know Brianna often picks on you, but in this case, *you* were the **antagonist**.

5. The wizard concocted a deadly poison for which there was no **antidote**.

6. The young singer hoped that her new music video would **propel** her to stardom.

7. If you complain to the community board about Mr. Murphy's noisy dog, he might **retaliate** by complaining about your aggressive cat.

8. He first claimed he had never even seen the cake, then later **contradicted** himself by admitting he had eaten a few slices.

9. The prince **professed** his love for Snow White and asked her to marry him.

10. If your truck breaks down in the middle of the road, it will **obstruct** traffic.

someone who acts against another	against or the opposite	to rule unfairly and keep from having power	to have deep care and concern for (something)	to get back at someone for wrongdoing	reserved; not inclined to talk
to speak the opposite of; to speak "against"	remedy or cure against something harmful	moving back gradually or slowly	to block or get in the way (of something)	to speak forth openly; to declare	to push or move forward

Roots Volume 1 — Lesson 4

> **STEP 3: Use Words in Sentences**
> For each sentence on the next page, fill in the word from the list that <u>best</u> fits the blank. *Note: Words may be used twice.*

Root	Word	Definition
RE back; again	**retaliate** (v) *retaliation* (n)	to get **back** at someone for a wrongdoing
	reticent (adj)	reserved; holding **back**; not inclined to talk
PRO for; forward	**profess** (v)	to speak **forth** openly; to declare
	propel (v) *propulsion* (n)	to push or move (something) **forward**
ANT/ ANTI against	**antagonist** (n) *antagonize* (v)	a bully, foe, or enemy; a person who takes unkind and unfair action **against** another
	antidote (n)	remedy or cure given **against** something harmful or unpleasant
CONTRA† against	**contradict** (v) *contradiction* (n) *contradictory* (adj)	to speak or represent the opposite of; to speak "**against**"
	contrary (adj) *contrarian* (n)	**against** or opposite; stubborn and inclined to disagree with others
OB/OP against	**obstruct** (v) *obstruction* (n)	to block or get in the way (of something) lit. to "build **against**"
	oppress (v) *oppression* (n) *oppressive* (adj)	to rule (people) in a harsh way and keep them from having power or opportunity; lit. to "press **against**"

---

† *Contra* also has an English form, **counter,** as in words like <u>counter</u>act and <u>counter</u>clockwise.

Roots Volume 1   Lesson 4

1. Since we knew that Aviva was _____ and timid, we were surprised when she signed up for the public speaking club.

2. Your statement _____ Tony's, so you cannot both be right.

3. We moved to higher ground so that the trees would not _____ our view.

4. Afraid he would _____ them, a group of townspeople met with the new sheriff and urged him to be compassionate.

5. We did not dislike the show -- on the _____, we loved it!

6. Joining a club or class is often a good _____ to loneliness.

7. Emily tried to _____ the path so that strangers could not get through.

8. If you _____ against your sister for breaking your toy, you will only make the situation worse.

9. They publicly _____ not to believe in the legend, but they tell me in private that they think it might be true.

10. Though he initially seemed to have no pulse, the steadfast paramedics were able to _____ him.

11. We are working on a new type of engine that can _____ race cars down the track even faster than before.

12. _____ to popular belief, the most expensive item is not always of the best quality.

13. Please don't _____ me in public. If you disagree with something I say, tell me privately afterward.

14. Most movie heroes prove their strength by prevailing against a tough _____.

40

Roots Volume 1

Lesson 4

> **STEP 4: Mixed Review**
> How much do you remember? Let's find out!

1. **Apathy** means "without feeling." What does **antipathy** mean?
    a. strong feeling for
    b. strong feeling against
    c. with feeling
    d. feeling again

2. *Essential* means "necessary." What does **nonessential** mean?
    a. necessary also
    b. not necessary
    c. necessary against
    d. necessary for

3. If something is **coherent**, it:
    a. makes sense
    b. makes no sense
    c. disturbs others
    d. blocks others

4. If two **colleagues** are **incompatible**, they:
    a. work well together
    b. work against each other
    c. do not work together
    d. do not work well together

5. An **interim** leader is one who:
    a. is only there for a time
    b. is harsh and cruel
    c. is rude and impolite
    d. is unimportant

6. **Circumvent** is to "go around" as **antiquated** is to:
    a. old-fashioned
    b. brand new
    c. go against
    d. push forward

7. An **intercultural** conversation is a conversation:
    a. with culture
    b. without culture
    c. between cultures
    d. around culture

8. "If we don't **win this tournament**, I will be shocked."
    a. disparage
    b. prevail
    c. forewarn
    d. retrogress

9. "Please try to **dispel** that ugly rumor."
    a. get rid of
    b. avoid
    c. spread
    d. prevent

10. Mr. Ullury wrote a memoir to keep his story alive for **future generations**.
    a. posterity
    b. posthumous
    c. nonentities
    d. colleague

Roots Volume 1   Lesson 4

11. What is least likely to be an **antecedent** to a toddler's temper tantrum?
    a. not getting a toy or treat
    b. seeing a rabbit
    c. dropping an ice cream cone
    d. having to go to bed

12. In _____, I'm glad we moved to this new town. If we hadn't, I would never have met my wonderful new friends!
    a. retrospect
    b. apathy
    c. retrogression
    d. posterity

13. Two years after Jack Rios died, his niece discovered a novel he had been writing and had it published _____.
    a. illogically
    b. unwittingly
    c. incompetently
    d. posthumously

14. Based on their prefixes, **retrogress** and **progress** are:
    a. synonyms
    b. antonyms
    c. unrelated

15. If you don't favor one side over the other, you are:
    a. impartial
    b. illogical
    c. incompetent
    d. apathetic

16. If you **circumnavigate** the world, you:
    a. go around it
    b. go to it
    c. go away from it
    d. go inside it

17. To **presume** is to make an assumption:
    a. beforehand
    b. after the fact
    c. without facts
    d. without feeling

18. Including second-language speakers, English is the world's most _____ language.
    a. beautiful
    b. widely-spoken
    c. unusual
    d. unpopular

19. Look at the suffixes. Which word is a **noun**?
    a. calcify
    b. perspicacity
    c. analogous
    d. emergent

20. Look at the suffixes. Which word is an **adjective**?
    a. confluence
    b. abdication
    c. grievous
    d. pedestrianize

Roots Volume 1 Lesson 4

> **STEP 5: Write the Words**
> Write each word one more time (in any order). Be sure to spell correctly!

> obstruct   contrary   propel   retaliate   profess
> contradict   reticent   antidote   oppress   antagonist

_____   _____

_____   _____

_____   _____

_____   _____

_____   _____

> **STEP 6: Dig a Little Deeper**
> Deepen and express your understanding in different ways.

1. Think of a book you have read (or a movie you have seen) in which a hero faces an *antagonist*. Who is the antagonist, and what is the struggle about? (Use the word *antagonist* in your response.)

2. Make up a sentence that correctly includes <u>two</u> words from the list. If you can't think of one single sentence, write two related sentences.

Roots Volume 1 — Lesson 4

> **STEP 7: Examine Other Words with the Same Prefix Roots**
> Check any words you already know well.
> Put an **X** next to words you do not know well or do not know at all.

RE	PRO	ANT/ANTI
☐ review	☐ project	☐ antacid
☐ recede	☐ proceed	☐ antibodies
☐ reveal	☐ process	☐ antimatter
☐ react	☐ proclivity	☐ antisocial
☐ resume	☐ proclaim	☐ antibiotic
☐ relive	☐ propensity	☐ antithesis
☐ regurgitate		☐ antipathy

CONTRA	OB/OP
☐ contraband	☐ obstinate
☐ contravene	☐ obscure
☐ controversy	☐ obdurate
	☐ oppose
	☐ opposite

> **STEP 8: Reflect on the Meaning of New Words**
> Choose two of the words that you do <u>not</u> already know and look up their meanings. Consider how the **root** in each word may relate to its meaning.

Word: Word:

Meaning: Meaning:

re	pro	ant/anti	contra	ob/op
back; again	for; forward	against	against	against

Roots Volume 1 Lesson 5

Lesson 5: Both, Many, All

ambi	multi	poly	omni	pan
both	many	many	all; every	all

multitude   omnipresence   pandemic   ambivalent   omnipotent
ambiguous   polytheistic   multifaceted   panacea   polyglot

STEP 1: Examine the Words
How well do you know them? What can you tell about them?

New Words *words I do not know; unfamiliar words*	Familiar Words *words I recognize but cannot fully define*	Known Words *words I understand but don't use often*	Mastered Words *words I know well and use regularly*

1. **Pandemic** and **polytheistic** share a suffix. Circle it.
   What part of speech does it suggest? _____

2. **Omnipotent** and **ambivalent** share a suffix. Circle it.
   What part of speech does it suggest? _____

3. The suffixes of **multitude** and **omnipresence** suggest what part of speech?
   a. noun   c. adjective
   b. verb   d. adverb

45

Roots Volume 1 — Lesson 5

> **STEP 2: Figure Out Meaning**
> Using context and your knowledge of roots, write the <u>sentence number</u> of the bolded word next to the best definition below. *Note: Not all definitions will be used.*

1. A true **polyglot**, Laura was fluent in French, Spanish, Arabic, and Chinese.

2. A **multitude** of fascinating plants and creatures lived in the underwater cave.

3. The captain's message was so **ambiguous** that we could not agree on whether he had ordered us to attack or retreat.

4. The new rule is sadly no **panacea**, though it has helped solve a few problems.

5. You don't have **omnipresence**, so you cannot be in two places at the same time.

6. Latisha was **ambivalent** about going to summer camp. She longed to make new friends, swim, and hike, but she hated the thought of being away from her family.

7. It was a **multifaceted** project that would take several steps to complete.

8. Hey, don't blame me for the rain – I'm not **omnipotent**!

9. Most ancient civilizations were **polytheistic**, often believing that each aspect of nature was controlled by a different god or goddess.

10. Doctors tried to halt the spread of the disease before it could become **pandemic**.

the ability to exist in all places at the same time	a large number	cure or remedy for all problems or illnesses	without blame or fault; innocent	involving many different parts or aspects	having two possible meanings; hard to interpret
widespread; spreading to all places	believing in many gods	having both feelings at the same time	to move slowly and carefully	all-powerful; having complete control	one who speaks many languages

Roots Volume 1 — Lesson 5

> **STEP 3: Use Words in Sentences**
> For each sentence on the next page, fill in the word from the list that best fits the blank. *Note: Words may be used twice.*

Root	Word	Definition
AMBI‡ both, two	**ambiguous** (adj) *ambiguity* (n)	having **two** possible meanings; unclear and hard to interpret
	ambivalent (adj) *ambivalence* (n)	having mixed feelings about something; having "**both**" feelings at the same time
MULTI many	**multifaceted** (adj)	involving **many** different parts or aspects; having many sides, as in cut gems
	multitude (n) *multitudinous* (adj)	a large number of things; a group of **many** people; the mass of ordinary people
POLY many	**polyglot** (n)	someone who can speak **many** languages
	polytheistic (adj) *polytheism* (n)	believing in more than one, or **many**, gods
OMNI all	**omnipotent** (adj) *omnipotence* (n)	**all**-powerful; having complete control or power
	omnipresence (n) *omnipresent* (adj)	the ability to exist in **all** places at the same time; the ability to be everywhere at once
PAN all	**panacea** (n)	a remedy for **all** problems or illnesses
	pandemic (adj) *pandemic* (n)	widespread; spreading to **all** places or affecting many people

---

‡ *Ambi* sometimes also appears as **amphi**, as in amphibians (animals that live in *both* land and water).

Roots Volume 1   Lesson 5

1. Walking away from the grave, Tara felt the _____ of her grandmother's spirit. It seemed to surround her completely, from the land, air, and sea.

2. I wanted to stay, but at the same time I longed to leave. My feelings could be described as utterly _____.

3. Looking out at the _____, David questioned whether he was brave enough to address such a large crowd.

4. Such a complicated problem will require a(n) _____ solution, not a simple fix.

5. After hearing all the evidence, the jury remained _____ about Ms. Harmon's guilt and could not decide whether to convict her.

6. A few knew the truth, but the _____ still believed the lie.

7. In 1918, a(n) _____ flu virus killed tens of millions of people.

8. No single strategy is going to be a(n) _____ for all your problems.

9. The little boy loved imagining he was a(n) _____ superhero who could defeat any antagonist.

10. Ethan hoped that by traveling to different countries and living among the local people, he would eventually become a(n) _____.

11. A(n) _____ of diseases can be caused by poor nutrition.

12. The majority of human religions throughout history have been _____, with a range of powerful deities and spirits.

13. Due to the _____ directions, half the students did the opposite of what the teacher intended.

14. The engagement ring featured a stunning _____ diamond.

15. If you could become a(n) _____ overnight, which languages would you choose to know?

Roots Volume 1 — Lesson 5

> **STEP 4: Mixed Review**
> How much do you remember? Let's find out!

1. If you experience **prejudice**, you experience being:
    a. bored and disinterested
    b. judged unfairly
    c. in agreement with someone
    d. fair and unbiased

2. To repress something is to keep it down by force. An <u>irrepressible</u> laugh:
    a. bursts forth openly
    b. stays inside
    c. fades quickly
    d. turns into a quiet chuckle

3. Because he lacked _____, Tom didn't bring warm enough clothes for the hike.
    a. apathy
    b. incompetence
    c. foresight
    d. posterity

4. Which two words have nearly <u>opposite</u> meanings:
    a. contradict and concur
    b. reticent and apathy
    c. nondescript and incompetent
    d. circuitous and interim

5. Someone treated like a **nonentity** might be:
    a. praised and celebrated
    b. ignored and overlooked
    c. welcomed openly
    d. taught good manners

6. If you are being <u>obstinate</u>, how do you respond when told to do something?
    a. you refuse to do it
    b. you don't care either way
    c. you do it eagerly
    d. you loudly agree

7. It's a lovely house, but I must *let you know in advance* that the basement floods.
    a. disparage you
    b. forewarn you
    c. foresight you
    d. prevail you

8. Antagonist is to friend/ally as **obstruct** is to:
    a. let pass through
    b. cure
    c. block or prevent
    d. disagree

9. If you are **reticent**, which are you <u>least</u> likely to do?
    a. profess your feelings
    b. believe in many gods
    c. foresee what will be needed
    d. oppress someone

Roots Volume 1 — Lesson 5

10. An *abridged* text is one that has been shortened. An **unabridged text**:
    a. has not been shortened
    b. has been lengthened
    c. is incomplete
    d. is unpopular

11. If someone's ideas are similar to yours, you are likely to:
    a. retaliate against them
    b. concur with them
    c. antagonize them
    d. disparage them

12. A seatbelt keeps you from _____ forward in the event of a crash.
    a. prevailing
    b. interceding
    c. retrogressing
    d. propelling

13. People who are being *oppressed* by an authority are likely to feel:
    a. contented and happy
    b. excited and enthusiastic
    c. frustrated and angry
    d. apathetic

14. **ANTEPASTO** REFERS TO A DISH EATEN:
    A. BEFORE THE MAIN MEAL
    B. WITH/DURING THE MAIN MEAL
    C. AFTER THE MAIN MEAL
    D. INSTEAD OF THE MAIN MEAL

15. Which of the following is NOT a likely reason for losing a debate?
    a. illogical reasoning
    b. incoherent speaking
    c. antiquated ideas
    d. prevailing ideas

16. *The Colonial period in America lasted roughly from 1492 to 1763. The **post**-Colonial period is:*
    a. the time from 1763 onward
    b. the time before 1492
    c. the end of the colonial period
    d. the beginning of the colonial period

17. To bode means to tell or hint at what is to come in the future. The word **forebode** therefore means:
    a. to hint at beforehand
    b. to hint at afterward
    c. to hint at quietly
    d. to hint at rudely

18. A **retroactive** rule applies:
    a. to past situations
    b. to future situations only
    c. to most situations
    d. to no situations

19. The vast majority of scientific and technical words in English have:
    a. Latin or Greek origins
    b. Germanic origins
    c. American origins
    d. Slavic origins

Roots Volume 1 — Lesson 5

> **STEP 5: Write the Words**
> Write each word one more time (in any order). Be sure to spell correctly!

> multitude   omnipresent   pandemic   ambivalent   omnipotent
> ambiguous   polytheistic   multifaceted   panacea   polyglot

---

> **STEP 6: Dig a Little Deeper**
> Deepen and express your understanding in different ways.

1. Make up a sentence that correctly includes <u>two</u> words from the list. If you can't think of one single sentence, write two related sentences.

2. The Ancient Greeks were **polytheistic**. Write down the names of three ancient Greek gods/goddesses and what each represented or was thought to control. (If you don't already know about Greek gods, look it up—it's fascinating!)

god/goddess	represents or controls

Roots Volume 1   Lesson 5

> **STEP 7: Examine Other Words with the Same Prefix Roots**
> Check any words you already know well.
> Put an **X** next to words you do not know well or do not know at all.

AMBI	MULTI	POLY
☐ ambidextrous	☐ multiplex	☐ polychromatic
☐ ambiparous	☐ multiply	☐ polycarbonate
☐ ambilateral	☐ multiple	☐ polygamy
☐ ambivert	☐ multifarious	☐ polytechnic
	☐ irresponsible	☐ polymorphic
	☐ irreversible	

OMNI	PAN
☐ omnivore	☐ pantheism
☐ omnibus	☐ panorama
☐ omnifarious	☐ pantheon
☐ omniscience	☐ pandemonium
	☐ panoply
	☐ panchromatic

> **STEP 8: Reflect on the Meaning of New Words**
> Choose two of the words that you do not already know and look up their meanings. Consider how the **root** in each word relates to its meaning.

Word: Word:

Meaning: Meaning:

ambi	**multi**	**poly**	**omni**	**pan**
both	many	many	all; every	all

Roots Volume 1 — Lesson 6

Lesson 6: More, Less, Half

super/sur	hyper	sub	hypo	semi
above; more	above; more	below	below	half

superlative   semiannual   subpar   hypercritical   subvert
hypothermia   hyperbole   surplus   hypocrisy   semiconscious

STEP 1: Examine the Words
How well do you know them? What can you tell about them?

New Words	Familiar Words	Known Words	Mastered Words
words I do not know; unfamiliar words	words I recognize but cannot fully define	words I understand but don't use often	words I know well and use regularly

1. Circle the suffix of **semiconscious**.
   What part of speech does it suggest? _____

2. Which two pairs of prefixes are SYNONYMS?

   _____ + _____   and   _____ + _____

3. **Hypo** and **hyper** are:
   a. synonyms
   b. antonyms
   c. unrelated

Roots Volume 1 — Lesson 6

> **STEP 2: Figure Out Meaning**
> Using context and your knowledge of roots, write the <u>sentence number</u> of the bolded word next to the best definition below. *Note: Not all definitions will be used.*

1. Though she always professed her commitment to honesty, her **hypocrisy** was revealed when we discovered she'd been lying to us for months.

2. When the cousins got lost in the snowy woods without winter coats, their parents worried they would develop **hypothermia**.

3. The charity ball is a **semiannual** affair, occurring every year in May and November.

4. Kyle's parents were disappointed in his **subpar** performance on the test.

5. There was a **surplus** of food after the harvest, so we gave away several boxes of fruit.

6. Luke was so excited when he met the famous marathon runner that he burst out in **hyperbole**: "You are the fastest being in the whole wide world, ever!"

7. Only **semi-conscious** after the fall, Emma lay on the ground mumbling incoherently.

8. If you weren't so **hypercritical**, you might notice the good things I do.

9. Isabella won recognition for her **superlative** efforts to raise money for charity.

10. The king ordered the army to arrest anyone plotting to **subvert** his power.

occurring once every half year; twice yearly	half-conscious; only partly aware	dangerously low body temperature	below the expected level or quality	an extra amount; more than needed	to undermine someone's authority; to overthrow
overly critical and disapproving	a deliberate statement of exaggeration	pretending to have good virtues one does not actually have	of the best quality; above all the rest	to speed quickly toward a goal	unusual and undesirable; bizarre

STEP 3: Use Words in Sentences
For each sentence on the next page, fill in the word from the list that <u>best</u> fits the blank. *Note: Words may be used twice.*

SUPER§/ SUR above; more	**superlative** (adj) *superlative (n)*	of the best quality; **above** (better than) all the rest
	surplus (n) *surplus (adj)*	an extra amount **above** what is needed; **more** than what is needed
HYPER above; more	**hyperbole** (n) *hyperbolic (adj)*	a word or statement of deliberate exaggeration (**above**/beyond the literal truth)
	hypercritical (adj) *hypercritically (adv)*	overly critical or disapproving; **more** critical than the situation warrants
SUB below; under	**subpar** (adj)	**below** the expected level or quality; not good enough
	subvert (adj) *subversion (n)*	to **undermine** (someone's authority); to overthrow (a powerful person or idea)
HYPO below; under	**hypocrisy** (n) *hypocrite (n)* *hypocritical (adj)*	pretending to have virtues one does not actually have; bad virtues **below** the surface; when one's actions and words contradict
	hypothermia (n)	body temperature that is dangerously **below** normal
SEMI half; partial	**semiconscious** (adj) *semiconsciously (adv)*	**half**-conscious; only partly aware
	semiannual (adj) *semiannually (adv)*	occurring every **half** year; twice yearly

---

§ *Super* sometimes also appears as **supr**, as in <u>supreme</u>.

Roots Volume 1 — Lesson 6

1. Josh was so popular that his yearly concert became a _____ show, held indoors in the winter and outdoors in the summer.

2. For hours after the surgery, Avery remained in a _____ state, not fully awakening until the following day.

3. In an attempt to _____ Mrs. Allen's authority, Bradley convinced several of his fellow classmates to deliberately disobey her rules.

4. After a _____ performance at the dance recital, Chelsea vowed to practice more regularly and improve her skill.

5. The rebel leaders worked secretly to _____ the emperor's oppressive government.

6. The candidate was accused of _____ for criticizing his opponent's tax cuts despite having himself proposed similar tax cuts a few weeks prior.

7. When Ellie said the play was the worst she had ever seen, we assumed that was _____ -- but when we saw the play, we realized she was right.

8. James bit his nails as his _____ older sister examined his essay on the life cycle of frogs. Had he finally written something good enough?

9. To prevent _____, wear warm clothing when hiking high in the mountains, even if the sun is shining.

10. Thanks to the budget _____, the city had enough money to take on new projects, such as creating two new parks and renovating the post office.

11. He had a _____ talent for organizing large events and was therefore the first person we called when we needed to plan a city-wide festival.

12. Her first novels were _____, but her later works were excellent.

13. It is _____ to say you believe in forgiveness while retaliating against everyone who offends you, even when they apologize.

14. I regret that because I was _____ of his efforts, Pedro stopped believing in himself and completely gave up.

Roots Volume 1

Lesson 6

> **STEP 4: Mixed Review**
> How much do you remember? Let's find out!

1. The **antithesis** of something is its:
   a. worth or value
   b. direct imitation
   c. movement forward
   d. complete opposite

2. To *inter* means "to bury in the earth." To **disinter** means:
   a. to bury with another
   b. to bury next to
   c. to bury under
   d. to dig up from the earth

3. *Morals* are a person's standards regarding right and wrong behavior and values. Someone who is **amoral**:
   a. has bad morals
   b. has no morals
   c. has many morals
   d. has all morals

4. Something that is **contrary** is:
   a. the opposite or against
   b. moving forward
   c. dull and ordinary
   d. temporary

5. If your ideas are **illogical**, they are:
   a. not rational or reasonable
   b. not successful
   c. old-fashioned or out of date
   d. the opposite of another's

6. Something that is **unambiguous**:
   a. is open to interpretation
   b. has one clear meaning
   c. is weak or has no power
   d. is simple or easy

7. The root *sci* has to do with knowing. Someone who is **omniscient**:
   a. knows all
   b. knows nothing
   c. knows before
   d. knows silently

8. Consider your answer to #7. Someone who is *omniscient* cannot also be:
   a. uncouth
   b. ambivalent
   c. contrary
   d. unwitting

9. Consider question #7 again. Someone who is **prescient** is someone who:
   a. knows all
   b. knows nothing
   c. knows before
   d. knows silently

Roots Volume 1   Lesson 6

10. Which of the following might be an *antidote* to sadness?
    a. being yelled at
    b. feeling unhappy
    c. visiting a friend
    d. feeling happy

11. English is a _____ language:
    a. Romance
    b. Slavic
    c. Germanic
    d. French

12. Which of the following does not require a **multifaceted** process?
    a. learning to play baseball
    b. waving hello
    c. planning a long trip
    d. presidential elections

13. The researchers dreamed of developing a _____ that could cure all infection.
    a. panacea
    b. pandemic
    c. polyglot
    d. prejudice

14. SOMETHING THAT IS OMNIPRESENT IS:
    A. EVERYWHERE
    B. NOWHERE
    C. NONEXISTENT
    D. UNPLEASANT

15. If you feel *ambivalent* about something, you may have thoughts that:
    a. contradict each other
    b. are posthumous
    c. are retaliatory
    d. retrogress

16. A *pandemic* is an illness or problem that:
    a. spreads widely
    b. disappears quickly
    c. affects only a few
    d. is usually fatal

17. Someone who demonstrates *incompetence* as a doctor might:
    a. be respected by colleagues
    b. win a prestigious award
    c. prescribe the wrong medication
    d. help cure many patients

18. *Multitude* and *retrospect*:
    a. are synonyms
    b. are both verbs
    c. are antonyms
    d. are unrelated

19. The root *morph* has to do with shape. Something **polymorphic**:
    a. can have many shapes
    b. has only one shape
    c. has an unusual shape
    d. can become any shape

Roots Volume 1   Lesson 6

> **STEP 5: Write the Words**
> Write each word one more time (in any order). Be sure to spell correctly!

> superlative   semiannual   subpar   hypercritical   subvert
> hypothermia   hyperbole   surplus   hypocrisy   semiconscious

_____   _____

_____   _____

_____   _____

_____   _____

_____   _____

> **STEP 6: Dig a Little Deeper**
> Deepen and express your understanding in different ways.

1. Think carefully. Which two words from the list are ANTONYMS? Write a sentence that includes both words.

2. Choose one word from the list (any word): _____
Draw a picture below to symbolize it or show what it means:

Roots Volume 1
Lesson 6

> **STEP 7: Examine Other Words with the Same Prefix Roots**
> Check any words you already know well.
> Put an **X** next to words you do not know well or do not know at all.

SUPER/SUR	HYPER	SUB
☐ supernatural	☐ hyperactive	☐ submarine
☐ supervise	☐ hypervigilant	☐ subway
☐ superficial	☐ hypertension	☐ subterranean
☐ surcharge	☐ hyperventilate	☐ subterfuge
☐ surcharge	☐ hypersensitive	☐ substitute
☐ surfeit		
☐ surmount		
☐ surtax		

HYPO	SEMI
☐ hypochondria	☐ semiformal
☐ hypothesis	☐ semiprecious
☐ hypotenuse	☐ semisweet
☐ hypothetical	

> **STEP 8: Reflect on the Meaning of New Words**
> Choose two of the words that you do not already know and look up their meanings. Consider how the **root** in each word relates to its meaning.

Word:

Meaning:

Word:

Meaning:

super/sur	hyper	sub	hypo	semi
above; more	above; more	below	below	half

Roots Volume 1 — Lesson 7

Lesson 7: Out, Away

ex/extr	e/ec	de	se	ab
out; outside	out; out of	away; down	away; apart	away

abscond   exodus   deduce   deprive   emit
segregate   abhor   secede   extricate   eccentric

STEP 1: Examine the Words
How well do you know them? What can you tell about them?

New Words words I do not know; unfamiliar words	Familiar Words words I recognize but cannot fully define	Known Words words I understand but don't use often	Mastered Words words I know well and use regularly

1. Circle the suffix of **eccentric**.
   What part of speech does it suggest? _____

2. *E/ec* and *ex/extr* are (circle one):   synonyms   antonyms   homophones

3. *De, se,* and *ab* are (circle one):   synonyms   antonyms   homophones

4. **Deduction**, a form of *deduce*, is what part of speech? _____

5. **Abhorrence** is what form of *abhor*? _____

Roots Volume 1 — Lesson 7

> **STEP 2: Figure Out Meaning**
> Using context and your knowledge of roots, write the sentence number of the bolded word next to the best definition below. *Note: Not all definitions will be used.*

1. It is cruel to **deprive** people of basic necessities such as food and water.

2. From the state of the trees, we quickly **deduced** that a tornado had struck the area.

3. Prior to the 1960s, some states and cities were legally allowed to **segregate** citizens based on race.

4. You should not stay in a job you **abhor**, even if it pays well.

5. The **eccentric** girl next door has twelve pet snakes and wears only purple clothing.

6. The criminals **absconded** before the police arrived on the scene.

7. Several countries threatened to **secede** from the alliance and form their own union.

8. The insect will **emit** a strange noise if you stroke its back.

9. The trapped animal tried desperately to **extricate** itself from the snare.

10. The invasion was followed by an **exodus** of families trying to escape to neighboring countries.

to break away or withdraw from	respected and admired	to take away from someone; to not give to someone	to figure out based on evidence; to infer	something unnecessary or unimportant	odd or strange; outside what is normal
to set apart (from others)	to hate or loathe	a mass departure; a large group leaving	to get out of (a difficult position or situation)	to send out or give off	to run away and hide; to flee from authority

Roots Volume 1 — Lesson 7

> **STEP 3: Use Words in Sentences**
> For each sentence on the next page, fill in the word from the list that <u>best</u> fits the blank. *Note: Words may be used twice.*

EX/EXTR outer; out	**exodus** (n)	a mass departure; a large group of people going **out** of or away from somewhere
	extricate (v) *extrication* (n)	to get (something or someone) **out** of a difficult position or situation
E/EC outside; out of	**eccentric** (adj) *eccentricity* (n)	odd or strange; **outside** what is considered normal in terms of behavior or customs
	emit (v) *emission* (n)	to send **out**; to give off
DE away; down	**deduce** (v) *deduction* (n)	to figure out through logic; to make an inference; to "take **away**" based on evidence
	deprive (v) *deprivation* (n)	to take something **away**; to not give something that should be given or is normally given
SE away; apart	**secede** (v) *secession* (n)	to break **away** from or withdraw from membership in a union or alliance
	segregate (v) *segregation* (n)	to set **apart** (from others)
AB away	**abhor** (v) *abhorrence* (n) *abhorrent* (adj)	to hate or loathe; (lit) to "shudder **away**" (from something)
	abscond (v)	to run **away** and hide; to flee or escape from authority

Roots Volume 1 — Lesson 7

1. I _____ violence and wish people would stop fighting.

2. She feared the stranger would _____ with the jewels, so she locked them in a chest near her bed.

3. After the flood, the city experienced a(n) _____ that reduced its population by half.

4. The Civil War began in 1861 when several Southern states voted to _____ from the United States.

5. Any second now, the machine will _____ a bright white light -- be sure to cover your eyes!

6. Though Tom had _____ habits and unusual mannerisms, his neighbors accepted him for who he was.

7. We must _____ ourselves from this unfortunate situation before it worsens.

8. Despite several clues, we were unable to _____ the identity of the mysterious stranger who donated a million dollars to the local homeless shelter.

9. When you _____ plants of light, they cannot grow.

10. Darius carefully _____ his hand from the sticky web.

11. If you _____ heat and humidity, don't move to Florida.

12. The school's decision to _____ younger students from older students in the lunchroom meant that Alice no longer saw her sister every day.

13. The clever thief _____ with dozens of expensive computers.

14. My doctor's office _____ sick patients from healthy ones to prevent the spread of illness.

Roots Volume 1

Lesson 7

> **STEP 4: Mixed Review**
> How much do you remember? Let's find out!

1. A *polytheist* is someone who:
   a. speaks many languages
   b. can change into many shapes
   c. believes in more than one god
   d. has no shape

2. A *nondescript* house might:
   a. be painted bright pink
   b. have an unusual shape
   c. have ornate stained glass windows
   d. be identical to other nearby houses

3. **Indo-European** refers to:
   a. the first English speakers
   b. a large language family
   c. the region where English originated
   d. Latin and Greek-based languages

4. <u>Hypertension</u> is a medical condition wherein one has:
   a. overly high blood pressure
   b. half the normal blood pressure
   c. not enough tension
   d. too low blood pressure

5. *Dexterity* refers to the ability to use one's hands skillfully. Someone who is <u>ambidextrous</u> is:
   a. unable to use either hand
   b. able to use only one hand
   c. able to use both hands skillfully
   d. unable to use both hands skillfully

6. *Scarcity* refers to a lack (not having enough of something). It can be an ANTONYM for:
   a. surplus
   b. hyperbole
   c. subpar
   d. superlative

7. After they attempted to break into the castle, the king _____ against the rebels by having their homes burned.
   a. contradicted
   b. retaliated
   c. professed
   d. forewarned

8. *Before* is to *after* as **ancestors** is to:
   a. retrogress
   b. posthumous
   c. posterity
   d. colleagues

9. "I'm so hungry I could eat a horse!" is an example of:
   a. hyperbole
   b. subversion
   c. hypocrisy
   d. surplus

Roots Volume 1 — Lesson 7

10. *We used to have a monthly potluck, but we've become so busy that now it's only a **twice yearly** affair.*
    - a. superlative
    - b. semiannual
    - c. subverted
    - d. surplus

11. *Though his first efforts were _____, with hard work he was able to produce _____ work.*
    - a. superlative . . . subpar
    - b. subpar . . . surplus
    - c. superlative . . . hypercritical
    - d. subpar . . . superlative

12. Which of the following would be ***irrelevant*** in an article on how to care for puppies?
    - a. what puppies eat
    - b. why puppies are cute
    - c. when puppies need to see a vet
    - d. how to keep puppies safe

13. Which is the most likely **antecedent** to getting in trouble?
    - a. having foresight
    - b. following bad advice
    - c. sadness
    - d. avoiding danger

14. SEMISWEET CHOCOLATE IS:
    - A. NOT TOO SWEET
    - B. OVERLY SWEET
    - C. NOT SWEET AT ALL
    - D. BITTER

15. If your behavior is ***uncouth***, you might be asked to:
    - a. visit more often
    - b. read more books
    - c. babysit a neighbor's child
    - d. leave a fancy restaurant

16. *Prejudice* and *hypocrisy* are:
    - a. synonyms
    - b. antonyms
    - c. unrelated in meaning
    - d. synonyms and antonyms

17. *To mingle is to mix. If you* comingle *different chemicals, you:*
    - a. separate them
    - b. mix them together
    - c. drink them
    - d. use them to develop a cure

18. *She was floating through **a vast empty hole** of space and time.*
    - a. a retrospect
    - b. an abyss
    - c. an intercession
    - d. an antecedent

19. Because his answer **went around in circles**, I did not trust that he was telling the truth.
    - a. circumvented
    - b. was obstructed
    - c. was circuitous
    - d. was unwitting

Roots Volume 1
Lesson 7

> **STEP 5: Write the Words**
> Write each word one more time (in any order). Be sure to spell correctly!

abscond   exodus   deduce   deprive   emit
segregate   abhor   secede   extricate   eccentric

_____   _____

_____   _____

_____   _____

_____   _____

_____   _____

> **STEP 6: Dig a Little Deeper**
> Deepen and express your understanding in different ways.

1. Based on your understanding of *hypothermia*, write a definition for **hyperthermia**.

2. Make up a sentence that correctly includes <u>two</u> words from the list. If you can't think of one single sentence, write two related sentences

Roots Volume 1   Lesson 7

> **STEP 7: Examine Other Words**
> Check any words you already know well.
> Put an **X** next to words you do not know well or do not know at all.

EX/EXTR	E/EC	DE
☐ exceed	☐ eject	☐ depressed
☐ exclude	☐ elude	☐ desist
☐ external	☐ effervescent	☐ dejected
☐ exuberant	☐ effusive	☐ demean
☐ exude		☐ degrade
☐ exhume		☐ devalue
☐ extraterrestrial		☐ descend
☐ extrapolate		☐ depart

SE	AB
☐ secrete	☐ absent
☐ sequester	☐ abbreviate
☐ seclude	☐ abrupt
☐ separate	☐ abject

> **STEP 8: Reflect on the Meaning of New Words**
> Choose two of the words that you do not already know and look up their meanings. Consider how the **root** in each word relates to its meaning.

Word:

Meaning:

Word:

Meaning:

ex/extr	e/ec	de	se	ab
out; outside	out; out of	away; down	away; apart	away

Roots Volume 1

Lesson 8

Lesson 8: In, Across, Through

in/im	intro/intra	en/em	trans	per
in; inside	into; inward	in; into	across	through

immerse   introspection   empathy   permeate   transmit
transient   introvert   enclose   internal   persevere

STEP 1: Examine the Words
How well do you know them? What can you tell about them?

New Words *words I do not know; unfamiliar words*	Familiar Words *words I recognize but cannot fully define*	Known Words *words I understand but don't use often*	Mastered Words *words I know well and use regularly*

1. Trans*ient* is what form of *transience*? _____

2. Internal*ly* is what form of *internal*? _____

3. Empath*ize* is what form of *empathy*? _____

4. Persever*ance* is what form of *persevere*? _____

5. Permeab*ility* is what form of *permeate*? _____

Roots Volume 1　　　　　　　　　　　　　　　　　　Lesson 8

> **STEP 2: Figure Out Meaning**
> Using context and your knowledge of roots, write the <u>sentence number</u> of the bolded word next to the best definition below. *Note: Not all definitions will be used.*

1. We dissected the mouse to learn about its **internal** organs.

2. Because Ava had broken her leg the year before, she had **empathy** for the boy hobbling up the stairs on crutches.

3. He was a **transient** person who never stayed in any place for more than a week.

4. Thick wires **transmit** electricity from the power plant to your home.

5. Without **introspection**, it is impossible to truly understand what motivates you.

6. We want to **enclose** the lobby with glass panes that will let light through while blocking wind and rain.

7. If you **immerse** yourself in a new language, you will pick it up more quickly.

8. When you face challenges, you must **persevere** in order to reach your goals.

9. People who are **introverts** sometimes feel anxious at large gatherings, like parties.

10. Sunlight **permeated** the curtain and cast a golden hue upon the floor.

to send, spread, or pass from one thing to another	not lasting long; not staying in one place or one condition	the ability to understand and share another's feelings	to pass or spread through	examining one's own thoughts; looking inward	to involve oneself completely; to dip completely (in liquid)
to experience fear or terror	a person who prefers being alone or who is very shy or reticent	to keep going through; to not give up	irresponsible; reckless; not giving thought to something	inner, inside; within one group or institution	to surround on all sides; to close in

Roots Volume 1 — Lesson 8

> **STEP 3: Use Words in Sentences**
> For each sentence on the next page, fill in the word from the list that <u>best</u> fits the blank. *Note: Words may be used twice.*

Prefix	Word(s)	Definition
IN/IM** in, inside, within	**internal** (adj) *internalize* (v)	inside; inner; within a group or institution
	immerse (v) *immersion* (n)	to involve oneself completely (**in** something); to dip completely (**in** liquid)
INTRO/INTRA inward, within	**introspection** (n) *introspective* (adj)	examining one's own thoughts and feelings; "looking **inward**" (mentally)
	introvert (n) *introverted* (adj)	one who often prefers being alone; one who is shy and reticent; *lit.* one who "turns **inward**"
EN/EM in, into	**enclose** (v) *enclosure* (n)	to surround on all sides; to close **in**
	empathy (n) *empathic* (adj) *empathize* (v)	the ability to understand or share someone else's feelings; the ability to imagine and care about how another person might feel; *lit.* "feeling **in**" with someone else
TRANS across, through	**transient** (adj) *transience* (n)	passing **through**; not lasting long; not staying in one place or in one condition
	transmit (v) *transmission* (n)	to spread, pass, or send **through** from one person or thing to another
PER across, through	**permeate** (v)	to pass or spread **through** something
	persevere (v) *perseverance* (n)	to keep going **through** despite challenges; to not give up

---

** Recall that IN and IM can also mean "not." You can often tell from the context of a word whether the prefix *in/im* means "in, into" or "not."

Roots Volume 1 — Lesson 8

1. The recipe says you should _____ the vegetables in boiling broth for five minutes.

2. If we can find the strength to _____, we might make it to the top of the mountain by nightfall.

3. After much _____, Dan realized that the misunderstanding had been partly his fault and that he should apologize.

4. The prince had been pampered his entire childhood and was never asked to consider anyone's needs besides his own. It was, therefore, no surprise that he lacked _____ for the sick and hungry subjects who begged for his aid.

5. Though she had no cuts or bruises, X-rays revealed she was suffering from _____ bleeding and would need to be hospitalized.

6. This is a(n) _____ matter and should not be discussed with anyone outside the organization.

7. A feeling of love _____ the room and made us all smile.

8. Always a(n) _____, Kaylie preferred to draw by herself rather than join the other children on the playground.

9. Though she abhorred the project and felt frustrated at every turn, Lisa found that listening to music gave her the courage to _____.

10. Fortunately, the toxic overgrowth in the pond is only a(n) _____ problem and will be resolved within a week.

11. The cold weather was severe but _____ and soon passed.

12. Through stories and songs, the village elders hoped to _____ their culture to the next generation.

13. When you are sick, avoid touching things before washing your hands so that you do not _____ disease to other people.

14. The witch decided to _____ the magic garden with a high wall in order to protect her potent herbs.

72

Roots Volume 1 — Lesson 8

> **STEP 4: Mixed Review**
> How much do you remember? Let's find out!

1. If something happens while you are **semiconscious**, you probably:
   a. feel both ways about it
   b. saw it beforehand
   c. are not aware of it at all
   d. do not remember it clearly

2. Someone who is a **polyglot** is likely to:
   a. be interested in other cultures
   b. be a good friend
   c. be unable to read
   d. be rude and impatient

3. The suffixes *–less* and *–ful*:
   a. are synonyms
   b. are antonyms
   c. both suggest nouns
   d. both suggest verbs

4. The root *duc* means "lead," so the word *seduce* means:
   a. to lead under
   b. to lead through
   c. to lead away
   d. not to lead

5. When something can be adapted to <u>all</u> musical harmonies, it is:
   a. semiharmonic
   b. subharmonic
   c. unharmonic
   d. panharmonic

6. To **propagate** an idea is to:
   a. put it forward and spread it
   b. speak out against it
   c. remain unaware of it
   d. hate it

7. I hope you don't **slide back** into your lazy habits.
   a. secede
   b. segregate
   c. retrogress
   d. propel

8. Tim Burgess died in 1967. In which year could his song have NOT been released if it was released **posthumously**?
   a. 2011
   b. 1942
   c. 1968
   d. 1979

9. To *foreshadow* an event is to:
   a. be unaware of it
   b. avoid it
   c. refuse to attend it
   d. hint at it beforehand

Roots Volume 1 — Lesson 8

10. *Superlative* is to *subpar* as **abhor** is to:
    a. hate
    b. like
    c. exodus
    d. avoid

11. *Ellen loved her _____ uncle despite his bizarre habits, for while he was strange, he had impeccable manners and was never _____ .*
    a. subpar . . . superlative
    b. eccentric . . . uncouth
    c. eccentric . . . surplus
    d. uncouth . . . eccentric

12. Someone who is **hypercritical** is prone to:
    a. criticizing things
    b. overheating
    c. exaggerating
    d. becoming too cold

13. Which is the opposite of *extricate*?
    a. get stuck in
    b. escape
    c. run away
    d. go around

14. IF YOU DEPRIVE SOMEONE OF THEIR POSSESSIONS, YOU:
    A. GIVE THEM BACK
    B. LEAVE THEM
    C. DISPARAGE THEM
    D. TAKE THEM AWAY

15. What have you been able to *figure out* from the clues left at the scene?
    a. deprive
    b. secede
    c. deduce
    d. extricate

16. The rock *gave off* a strange glow, and we sensed it was magical.
    a. emitted
    b. professed
    c. propelled
    d. forewarned

17. Which is most likely to cause an *exodus* from a large city?
    a. famine and widespread hunger
    b. reduced crime and violence
    c. friendly inhabitants
    d. a popular new mayor

18. If you're reading about **post**-*war* Britain, you're reading about Britain:
    a. before the war
    b. after the war
    c. during the war
    d. against the war

19. A *colleague* is:
    a. someone with whom you work
    b. someone who blocks progress
    c. someone who is partly aware
    d. someone who speaks badly of you

Roots Volume 1 Lesson 8

> **STEP 5: Write the Words**
> Write each word one more time (in any order). Be sure to spell correctly!

> immerse   introspection   empathy   permeate   transmit
> transient   introvert   enclose   internal   persevere

_____   _____

_____   _____

_____   _____

_____   _____

_____   _____

> **STEP 6: Dig a Little Deeper**
> Deepen and express your understanding in different ways.

Using the words **persevere** and **prevail**, write a paragraph about a time you had to keep going despite challenges. (Tell a true story, or invent one!)

Roots Volume 1 — Lesson 8

> **STEP 7: Examine Other Words**
> Check any words you already know well.
> Put an **X** next to words you do not know well or do not know at all.

IN/IM	INTRO/INTRA	EN/EM
☐ internal	☐ introduce	☐ engross
☐ inner	☐ intromit	☐ enfold
☐ inside	☐ introject	☐ enliven
☐ imbibe	☐ intramural	☐ embody
☐ imbue	☐ intravenous	☐ embolden

TRANS	PER
☐ transfer	☐ perforate
☐ transparent	☐ perceive
☐ translucent	☐ perceptive
☐ intransigent	☐ imperceptible
☐ transport	☐ percolate

> **STEP 8: Reflect on the Meaning of New Words**
> Choose two of the words that you do not already know and look up their meanings. Consider how the *root* in each word relates to its meaning.

Word:

Meaning:

Word:

Meaning:

in/im	intro/intra	en/em	trans	per
in; inside	into; inward	in; into	across	through

Roots Volume 1 — Lesson 9

Lesson 9: Same and Different

syn/sym	homo	equ	hetero	altr/alter
together	same	same, equal	different	other

equivalent   homophone   equitably   homogeneous   altruism
heterogeneous   altercation   synthesis   heterodox   symbiotic

Step 1: Examine the Words
How well do you know them? What can you tell about them?

New Words	Familiar Words	Known Words	Mastered Words
words I do not know; unfamiliar words	words I recognize but cannot fully define	words I understand but don't use often	words I know well and use regularly

1. Circle the suffix of **altruism**.
   What part of speech does it suggest? _____

2. **Altruis*tic*** is what form of *altruism*? _____

3. Which **four** words from the list have suffixes that suggest they are **adjectives**?

   _____   _____

   _____   _____

Roots Volume 1 — Lesson 9

> **STEP 2: Figure Out Meaning**
> Using context and your knowledge of roots, write the <u>sentence number</u> of the bolded word next to the best definition below. *Note: Not all definitions will be used.*

1. Tara was careful to distribute the candy **equitably**, ensuring that each guest received exactly three pieces.

2. The **synthesis** of ancient ideas and new technology can sometimes lead to the best inventions.

3. *See* and *sea* are well-known **homophones**.

4. Ants and aphids have a **symbiotic** relationship, with the ants gaining the aphids' milk and the aphids gaining protection from predators.

5. In a **homogeneous** study group, all students are on the same level.

6. In a **heterogeneous** study group, students are of different levels or abilities.

7. The two vacuum cleaners look different, but in terms of power they are **equivalent**.

8. His **altruism** led him to pursue a job at a homeless shelter, even though it paid little.

9. James's **heterodox** ideas contradicted the advice of the respected village elders.

10. On the way home we witnessed an **altercation** between two angry people.

living together to each other's benefit	fairly; treating all parties equally	a word that sounds the same but has a different meaning	of the same kind or type	combining together to make something new	to hope fervently; to long for; to wish
of the same worth, function, or amount	selfish and greedy; miserly	different from what is considered acceptable	unselfish concern for others	of different types or parts; not all the same	loud argument or dispute

Roots Volume 1 — Lesson 9

> **STEP 3: Use Words in Sentences**
> For each sentence on the next page, fill in the word from the list that <u>best</u> fits the blank. *Note: Words may be used twice.*

SYN/SYM same, together	**synthesis** (n) *synthesize (v)*	the combining of parts to make a whole; putting different elements or ideas **together** to make something new
	symbiotic (adj) *symbiosis (n)*	living **together** to each other's benefit; benefiting both sides in a relationship
HOMO same	**homogeneous** (adj) *homogeneity (n)* *homogeneously (adv)*	all of the **same** type or quality; without variety or difference
	homophone (n)	a word having the **same** pronunciation as another word but with a different meaning
EQU same	**equitably** (adv) *equitable (adj)*	fairly; treating all sides the **same** (equally)
	equivalent (adj) *equivalent (n)* *equivalence (n)*	of the **same** amount, worth, or function
HETERO different	**heterodox** (adj) *heterodoxy (n)*	having **different** ideas or beliefs from what is considered acceptable or standard
	heterogeneous (adj) *heterogeneity (n)* *heterogeneously (adv)*	made up of **different** types or qualities; not all made up of the same thing; diverse
ALTR/ALTER other	**altruism** (n) *altruistic (adj)*	unselfish concern for the well-being of **other** people
	altercation (n)	a noisy dispute or conflict with **another**

Roots Volume 1   Lesson 9

1. 90% and A- are _____ scores on most tests and assignments.

2. The teacher divided the class into _____ groups so that students who understood the material could help those students needing more help.

3. The new proposal was considered too _____ to be approved by the council leader, a staunch traditionalist.

4. Through the _____ of several materials, a new type of cloth was developed.

5. Aaron enjoyed meeting people from all over the world and was disappointed to find that the "international" summer camp was actually very _____.

6. Please control your temper. We don't want any _____ here!

7. The mayor pledged to ensure that education funds would be distributed _____ among all schools.

8. A good way to avoid a(n) _____ is for both sides to talk through their disagreement calmly and listen to what the other has to say.

9. *Bear* and *bare* are _____.

10. Raised in a(n) _____ family, Isabel had been taught from an early age to question the cultural norms of her community.

11. Bart and Barry had a(n) _____ study partnership; Bart helped Barry with math, and Barry helped Bart with writing.

12. Mrs. Wong, who continued to serve orphaned children even when she became ill, was honored for her extraordinary _____.

13. Healthy fats are important in the _____ of new brain cells.

14. Alarmed by her selfish and greedy tendencies, Maddie's parents hoped she would eventually develop a sense of empathy and _____.

Roots Volume 1

Lesson 9

> **Step 4: Mixed Review**
> How much do you remember? Let's find out!

1. *Secede* is the ANTONYM of:
   a. leave
   b. join
   c. love
   d. hate

2. A person with **multifarious** hobbies has:
   a. extra hobbies
   b. no hobbies
   c. many hobbies
   d. few hobbies

3. If your refrigerator's cooling system is **antiquated**, it might be more likely to:
   a. keep things very cold
   b. heat things up
   c. stop working soon
   d. run perfectly

4. If something is *transient*, you should:
   a. not expect it to last long
   b. spread or pass it along
   c. surround it on all sides
   d. become deeply involved in it

5. What is something that **introspection** might NOT lead someone to realize?
   a. who is behind the door
   b. how they study best
   c. why they feel sad sometimes
   d. what they want most in life

6. Which are you most likely to want to **circumvent**?
   a. a new boat
   b. a clean, sunny park
   c. an unfair rule
   d. an old friend

7. Which pair is most likely to be **compatible**?
   a. a chicken and a rooster
   b. an elephant and a hamster
   c. a tiger and a rabbit
   d. a goldfish and a pigeon

8. What is a likely cause for someone to **disparage** another?
   a. hope
   b. boredom
   c. love
   d. anger

9. *Mobile* means "able to move." **Immobile** therefore means:
   a. able to move under
   b. not able to move
   c. able to move forwards
   d. able to move backwards

10. *Hypothermia* is to *hyperthermia* as **segregate** is to:
    a. disparage
    b. unite
    c. separate
    d. prejudice

Roots Volume 1 — Lesson 9

11. If you *transmit* something, you:
    a. pass it along
    b. go through it
    c. push it through
    d. pass over it

12. Which of the following human organs is NOT *internal*?
    a. brain
    b. stomach
    c. skin
    d. all of the above

13. It is impossible to be both:
    a. omnipotent + incompetent
    b. contrary + prejudiced
    c. coherent + antiquated
    d. reticent + oppressed

14. THERE IS A 30-MINUTE GAP BETWEEN THE TWO PERFORMANCES. WHAT SHOULD WE DO IN BETWEEN?
    A. IN THE INTERIM
    B. PREVAILING
    C. INTERCEDING
    D. IN RETROSPECT

15. To *restrain* is to hold (someone/something) back. Which word means the opposite?
    a. deduce
    b. deprive
    c. propel
    d. concur

16. *Ven* is a Latin root meaning *come*. To **convene** is to:
    a. come through
    b. not come
    c. come apart
    d. come together

17. Which term is a synonym for *panacea*?
    a. cure-all
    b. all-knowing
    c. all-consuming
    d. all-purpose

18. If an agreement is *binding*, you have to stick to it. A non-binding agreement is one you:
    a. can get out of
    b. never agree to
    c. must always stick to
    d. are unaware of

19. If you *immerse* yourself in something, you:
    a. hate to do it
    b. don't know much about it
    c. cover it up
    d. become deeply involved in it

Roots Volume 1
Lesson 9

> **STEP 5: Write the Words**
> Write each word one more time (in any order). Be sure to spell correctly!

> equivalent homophone equitably homogeneous altruism
> heterogeneous altercation synthesis heterodox symbiotic

_____   _____

_____   _____

_____   _____

_____   _____

> **STEP 6: Dig a Little Deeper**
> Deepen and express your understanding in different ways.

1. Using your knowledge of the word *introvert* and the root *ex/extr*, write a definition for the word **extrovert**.

2. Write a short paragraph on any topic (fiction or non-fiction) that correctly uses <u>at least three words</u> from Lesson 9. Be imaginative! Have fun! *Note: Feel free to write below or use separate paper, or you may type your paragraph.*

Roots Volume 1 Lesson 9

> **STEP 7: Examine Other Words**
> Check any words you already know well.
> Put an **X** next to words you do not know well or do not know at all.

SYN/SYM	HOMO	EQU
☐ synergy	☐ homonym	☐ equal
☐ symbol	☐ homozygous	☐ equality
☐ photosynthesis	☐ homologous	☐ equity
☐ synchronize	☐ homology	☐ equilibrium
☐ "in sync"	☐ homomorphic	☐ equilateral
☐ synagogue		

HETERO	ALTR/ALTER
☐ heterozygous	☐ alternate
☐ heterologous	☐ alternative
☐ heterochromatic	☐ alter

> **STEP 8: Reflect on the Meaning of New Words**
> Choose two of the words that you do not already know and look up their meanings. Consider how the **root** in each word relates to its meaning.

Word: Word:

Meaning: Meaning:

syn/sym together	**homo** same	**equ** same, equal	**hetero** different	**altr/alter** other

84

Roots Volume 1 — Lesson 10

Lesson 10: Good, Right, True

ben/bene	bon	eu	rect	ver
good	good	good	right	true

benefit rectify bonanza euphemism bona fide
rectitude euphoria verify veracity benevolent

Step 1: Examine the Words
How well do you know them? What can you tell about them?

New Words	Familiar Words	Known Words	Mastered Words
words I do not know; unfamiliar words	words I recognize but cannot fully define	words I understand but don't use often	words I know well and use regularly

1. **Rectify** and **verify** share a suffix. Circle it.
   What part of speech does it suggest? _____

2. What part of speech is suggested by the suffix of **euphemism**? _____

3. **Beneficial** is what form of *benefit*? _____

4. What part of speech is suggested by the suffix of **benevolent**? _____

5. What part of speech is suggested by the suffix of **veracity**? _____

85

Roots Volume 1

Lesson 10

> **STEP 2: Figure Out Meaning**
> Using context and your knowledge of roots, write the <u>sentence number</u> of the bolded word next to the best definition below. *Note: Not all definitions will be used.*

1. We approved the new policy after we were assured it would **benefit** everyone.

2. "Pass away" is a common **euphemism** for *die*.

3. We had heard that it was a dangerous place full of hostile people, but everyone we met was **benevolent** and welcoming.

4. Because of his history of lying, we did not trust the **veracity** of his statements.

5. The situation is terrible, and someone needs to **rectify** it immediately.

6. The **euphoria** she felt when she won the competition can hardly be described.

7. Bruce's strong sense of **rectitude** prevented him from participating in the burglary.

8. Lab tests showed that the gemstone was a **bona fide** ruby worth a fortune.

9. The movie was a big hit and a **bonanza** for local movie theaters, which had been struggling to attract patrons.

10. Before I give you access to the safe, can you **verify** that you are the rightful owner?

morally right and good behavior and ideas	to fix and make right again	anger or rage; fury	truthfulness; accuracy	to do good for; to help or assist	strong good feelings; intense joy
good and kind; harmless	an event or situation that leads to something good	to prove to be true; to check that something is true	to cause pain, suffering, or sorrow	a good or polite way of expressing something unpleasant	real and genuine; in "good faith"

86

Roots Volume 1 — Lesson 10

> **STEP 3: Use Words in Sentences**
> For each sentence on the next page, fill in the word from the list that <u>best</u> fits the blank. *Note: Words may be used twice.*

BEN/BENE good	**benefit** (v) *benefit* (n) *beneficial* (adj)	to do **good** for; to help or assist; to promote or improve one's position or well-being
	benevolent (adj) *benevolence* (n)	kind and with **good** intentions
BON good	**bona fide** (adj)	real and genuine; in "**good** faith" (can be trusted)
	bonanza (n)	a large amount of something **good**; an event or situation that leads to **good** fortune
EU good	**euphemism** (n) *euphemistic* (adj)	a **good** or polite way of expressing something embarrassing or unpleasant
	euphoria (n) *euphoric* (adj)	strong **good** feelings; intense joy and happiness
RECT right	**rectify** (v) *rectification* (n)	to fix a situation and make it **right** again
	rectitude (n)	morally **right** behavior and ideas
VER true	**verify** (v) *verification* (n)	to check whether something is **true**; to prove that something is **true**
	veracity (n)	**truthfulness**; accuracy

Roots Volume 1 — Lesson 10

1. I hope this new technology will _____ many people throughout the world.

2. Though her appearance was alarming and even frightening, the woman next door was completely _____.

3. After its television ad aired, the charity received a(n) _____ of donations.

4. Your apology is appreciated, but this is a dilemma you cannot _____ with words alone.

5. Suspicious of the article's claims, Eve decided to _____ the facts for herself before including them in her report.

6. It may seem an unlikely story, but I was there when it happened and can vouch for the _____ of his account.

7. Mia's distress turned to _____ when she realized her grandmother's ring was not lost after all.

8. Brandon, unable to think of a(n) _____ to soften his statement, finally confessed: "I farted."

9. The opening of the new museum was a(n) _____ for the town's residents, whose businesses prospered under the flood of tourists.

10. Though respected for his broad knowledge, Mr. Pilotti was not considered a(n) _____ doctor because he had never finished medical school.

11. People should not share sensational news reports online without first _____ that they are true.

12. He was a man of great _____ and honesty, trusted by all.

13. Please find a way to _____ the problems obstructing our progress.

14. What appeared to be junk was actually a(n) _____ treasure, valued at over a million dollars.

Roots Volume 1

Lesson 10

> **STEP 4: Mixed Review**
> How much do you remember? Let's find out!

1. If you have **empathy** for someone, you can imagine how they:
   a. think
   b. feel
   c. work
   d. none of the above

2. Someone with **heterodox** ideas has ideas that _____ what is generally accepted or approved of.
   a. permeate
   b. concur with
   c. are compatible with
   d. are contrary to

3. I know you face challenges, but you must _____ despite them or you will never _____.
   a. prevail . . . immerse
   b. permeate . . . persevere
   c. immerse . . . persevere
   d. persevere . . . prevail

4. Which is a *homophone* for INSTANCE?
   a. instant
   b. instantly
   c. instants
   d. instances

5. Because he was _____ and never took sides, we trusted him to divide the property _____.
   a. impartial . . . equivalent
   b. equivalent . . . altruistically
   c. impartial . . . equitably
   d. altruistic . . . benevolent

6. They were so **closed off** in their own community that they rarely made friends from other places.
   a. enclosed
   b. immersed
   c. homogeneous
   d. introverted

7. The culture of violence was ____ and ____ every city in the region.
   a. panacea . . . permeated
   b. pandemic . . . permeated
   c. permeated . . . pandemic
   d. pandemic . . . panacea

8. The police might need to **intercede** when there is a(n):
   a. rectitude
   b. antecedent
   c. altercation
   d. multitude

9. To **dispel** something is to:
   a. make it go away
   b. cause it to spread
   c. speak badly about it
   d. go around it

Roots Volume 1 — Lesson 10

10. Something that is *pervasive* is:
    a. internal
    b. external
    c. eccentric
    d. widespread

11. In a *homogeneous* group, everyone is:
    a. uncouth
    b. unwitting
    c. similar or the same
    d. different

12. Animals that have a *symbiotic* relationship must be:
    a. heterogeneous
    b. compatible
    c. subpar
    d. equivalent

13. If you have *foresight*, you can:
    a. predict what might be needed
    b. see the past
    c. speak against something
    d. speak many languages

14. **THE ROOT RETRO MEANS:**
    A. FORWARDS
    B. ANCIENT
    C. BACKWARDS
    D. OLD-FASHIONED

15. *Terr* is a Latin root for "earth." Something *subterranean* is:
    a. not from Earth
    b. made of earth/clay
    c. underground
    d. above ground

16. After snatching the crown, the wicked elf ____ to the hills.
    a. seceded
    b. absconded
    c. exodus
    d. extricated

17. *Altruism* is to *selfish* as *kindness* is to:
    a. quiet
    b. afraid
    c. mean
    d. generous

18. Life seemed to be crumbling around Lola, but for some odd reason she *just didn't care*.
    a. was reticent
    b. was apathetic
    c. was unwitting
    d. was irrelevant

19. English has so many Latin/Greek root words because Latin:
    a. was widely used in medieval Britain
    b. is an easy-to-understand language
    c. is Indo-European
    d. is Germanic

Roots Volume 1   Lesson 10

> **STEP 5: Write the Words**
> Write each word one more time (in any order). Be sure to spell correctly!

> benefit   rectify   bonanza   euphemism   bona fide
> rectitude   euphoria   verify   veracity   benevolent

_____   _____

_____   _____

_____   _____

_____   _____

_____   _____

> **STEP 6: Dig a Little Deeper**
> Deepen and express your understanding in different ways.

Make up a fictional character who represents all things good and true. Write a short paragraph about him/her using as many words from the list as possible (at least three).

Roots Volume 1 — Lesson 10

> **STEP 7: Examine Other Words**
> Check any words you already know well.
> Put an **X** next to words you do not know well or do not know at all.

BEN/BENE	BON	EU
☐ beneficial	☐ bonbon	☐ euphonious
☐ benediction	☐ bonhomie	☐ euphonium
☐ benign	☐ *bon voyage*	☐ eudemonia
	☐ *bon appetit*	☐ eulogy
	The words in italics are French terms commonly used by English speakers.	

RECT	VER
☐ rectifiable	☐ very
☐ rectifier	☐ verily
☐ correct	☐ veritable
☐ rectangle	☐ verisimilitude
	☐ verdict

> **STEP 8: Reflect on the Meaning of New Words**
> Choose two of the words that you do not already know and look up their meanings. Consider how the **root** in each word relates to its meaning.

Word:

Meaning:

Word:

Meaning:

ben/bene	bon	eu	rect	ver
good	good	good	right	true

Roots Volume 1 — Lesson 11

Lesson 11: Bad, Wrong, False

dys	**mal**	**err**	**mis**	**fall/fals**
bad; difficult	bad	wrong	wrong; bad	false

erroneous dysfunctional fallacy malevolent dystopia
misgivings malady falsify aberration misconstrue

Step 1: Examine the Words
How well do you know them? What can you tell about them?

New Words *words I do not know; unfamiliar words*	Familiar Words *words I recognize but cannot fully define*	Known Words *words I understand but don't use often*	Mastered Words *words I know well and use regularly*

1. Based on the suffix, what part of speech is **erroneous**? _____

2. Based on the suffix, what part of speech is **falsify**? _____

3. Based on the suffix, what part of speech is **aberration**? _____

4. **Malevolent** is what form of *malevolence*? _____

5. **Dysfunctional** is what form of *dysfunction*? _____

Roots Volume 1 — Lesson 11

> **STEP 2: Figure Out Meaning**
> Using context and your knowledge of roots, write the <u>sentence number</u> of the bolded word next to the best definition below. *Note: Not all definitions will be used.*

1. Your report is full of **erroneous** information; please check the sources again carefully.

2. It is illegal to **falsify** a signature on an official document.

3. Speak coherently so that others do not **misconstrue** your statements.

4. We shuddered when he curved his wicked mouth into a **malevolent** smile.

5. The bubonic plague was a dreadful **malady** with painful symptoms.

6. The novel was set in a futuristic **dystopia** where people were taken from their parents at birth and raised to be robotic workers for the government.

7. Allegra's low score on the math quiz was an **aberration**, for she usually earned perfect marks.

8. Lee had serious **misgivings** about our plan to decorate the bathroom with nail polish.

9. We were disappointed to learn that his story of being rescued while mountain climbing was a complete **fallacy**, made up on the spot.

10. The town's bus service was so **dysfunctional** that riders could not be sure when a bus might come or even which route it might take.

interpret wrongly	doubts or bad feelings about something	wrong; false	to pass or spread through	to hope something will improve	to change something and make it false or fake
functioning badly; not working properly	lie; falsehood; mistaken belief	evil; with bad intentions	something that is unusual in a bad way	frightening or bad community or society	illness; bad health

Roots Volume 1 — Lesson 11

> **STEP 3: Use Words in Sentences**
> For each sentence on the next page, fill in the word from the list that best fits the blank. *Note: Words may be used twice.*

Root	Word	Definition
DYS bad; difficult	**dysfunctional** (adj) *dysfunction* (n)	working or functioning **badly**; not working properly
	dystopia (n) *dystopian* (adj)	a society or community that is **bad** and frightening (often fictional or imaginary)
MAL bad	**malady** (n)	an illness; **bad** health
	malevolent (adj) *malevolence* (n)	evil; with **bad** intentions
ERR wrong, bad	**erroneous** (adj) *erroneously* (adv)	**wrong** or mistaken
	aberration (n) *aberrant* (adj)	something that is unusual or expected in a **bad** way
MIS wrong, bad	**misconstrue** (v)	to interpret **wrongly**; to come to **wrong** understanding of something
	misgivings (n)	doubts or second thoughts; **bad** feelings about how something is going or will go
FALL/FALS false	**fallacy** (n) *fallacious* (adj)	something **false** or untrue; a mistaken belief
	falsify (v)	to change something and make it **false** or fake; to prove that something is false

Roots Volume 1   Lesson 11

1. Andrew's aunt urged him to ignore the _____ that wealth buys happiness and to focus as much energy on making friends as on making money.

2. Paulina spoke so clearly and eloquently that no one could _____ her message.

3. When he heard about the strange _____ afflicting residents in his city, Grayson felt compelled to find a cure.

4. In the nightmare, Ellen was lost in a bizarre _____ where no one smiled and everything was grey and cold.

5. The jury's _____ decision to convict Ian Greene was overturned when he appealed and was able to prove his innocence.

6. Was his slow time in the race a(n) _____, or does he always come in last?

7. The surgeon attempted to dispel any _____ his patients had about the use of the new laser surgery methods.

8. Because she had _____ her friend's words, Rosa thought she had been excluded from the party when in fact she had been invited.

9. Though it is important to be careful, most people you meet are not _____ and do not wish you any harm.

10. The corrupt scientist _____ the results of the study to show that the new substance was safe when in fact it had been shown to be toxic.

11. Without good leadership and a clear mission, any organization is likely to become disorganized and _____.

12. The class debated whether the mysterious character was kind-hearted and altruistic or _____ and cold.

13. If you have any _____ about the upcoming trip, please let us know so we can discuss it before we leave.

Roots Volume 1

Lesson 11

> **STEP 4: Mixed Review**
> How much do you remember? Let's find out!

1. English is a _____ language.
    a. Slavic
    b. Celtic
    c. Romance
    d. Germanic

2. **Comedian is to *funny* as NONENTITY is to:**
    a. boring or dull
    b. unimportant
    c. famous
    d. polite

3. Please *let us know in advance* about any risks involved in this mission.
    a. intercede us
    b. prevail us
    c. forewarn us
    d. foresight us

4. To <u>profess</u> something is to:
    a. avoid it
    b. hold it back
    c. believe in it
    d. state it aloud

5. Someone who is **reticent** is not likely to:
    a. talk openly
    b. give or share
    c. be fair or just
    d. do a good job

6. **In the fairytale Snow White, the <u>antagonist</u> is:**
    a. Snow White
    b. the chief dwarf
    c. the prince
    d. the wicked stepmother

7. If a group of people is **oppressed**, they do not have:
    a. many friends
    b. power or influence
    c. a cure
    d. fame or celebrity

8. If something is embarrassing or unpleasant for you, you might use a(n) ____ to describe it.
    a. euphemism
    b. altercation
    c. euphoria
    d. altruism

9. Which is most likely to **benefit** someone who is very tired?
    a. running a race
    b. a headache
    c. being weary
    d. a long nap

Roots Volume 1   Lesson 11

10. Something that is ***bona fide*** is:
    a. untrue
    b. wrong
    c. real and genuine
    d. good or kind

11. Can you **check that he is who he says he is**?
    a. falsify his identity
    b. rectify his identity
    c. transmit his identity
    d. verify his identity

12. If you are experiencing ***apathy***, then you are NOT experiencing:
    a. euphoria
    b. prejudice
    c. synthesis
    d. a fallacy

13. If two people are having an ***altercation***, a third person might ***intercede*** in order to:
    a. circumvent the problem
    b. rectify the situation
    c. deprive others
    d. prevent a pandemic

14. IF SOMETHING IS <u>ILLOGICAL</u> IT:
    A. DOES NOT MAKE SENSE
    B. IS COHERENT
    C. SUBVERTS AUTHORITY
    D. PERMEATES AN AREA

15. Someone who is ***<u>apolitical</u>*** is:
    a. not interested in politics
    b. very political
    c. works under a politician
    d. works with politicians

16. To *revoke* something is to end or stop it. Something ***<u>irrevocable</u>***:
    a. might be ended or stopped
    b. has already been ended or stopped
    c. cannot be ended or stopped
    d. must be ended or stopped

17. Mr. Tiro admitted he had taken the money, but he was found not guilty because he had taken it _____.
    a. ambivalently
    b. in retrospect
    c. coherently
    d. unwittingly

18. *Fluent* can mean "flowing." Something ***<u>circumfluent</u>***:
    a. flows through
    b. flows around
    c. flows under
    d. flows above

19. *Posthumous* is to *"after death"* as VERACITY is to:
    a. falsehood
    b. truthfulness
    c. proof
    d. evidence

Roots Volume 1 — Lesson 11

STEP 5: Write the Words
Write each word one more time (in any order). Be sure to spell correctly!

> erroneous   dysfunctional   fallacy   malevolent   dystopia
> misgivings   malady   falsify   aberration   misconstrue

STEP 6: Dig a Little Deeper
Deepen and express your understanding in different ways.

Make up an **evil character** and write a paragraph about him or her using as many words from Lesson 11 as you can (at least three). Underline the words as you use them.

Roots Volume 1 — Lesson 11

> **STEP 7: Examine Other Words**
> Check any words you already know well.
> Put an **X** next to words you do not know well or do not know at all.

DYS	MAL	ERR
☐ dyspepsia	☐ malcontent	☐ error
☐ dyslexia	☐ malicious	☐ err
☐ dyspraxia	☐ malignant	☐ inerrant
☐ dyscalculia	☐ malaise	
	☐ malefactor	
	☐ dismal	
	☐ abysmal	

MIS	FALL/FALS
☐ misanthrope	☐ false
☐ mistake	☐ fallacious
☐ misspell	☐ falsehood
☐ misplace	☐ falsetto
☐ misunderstand	

> **STEP 8: Reflect on the Meaning of New Words**
> Choose two of the words that you do not already know and look up their meanings. Consider how the *root* in each word relates to its meaning.

Word:

Meaning:

Word:

Meaning:

dys	mal	err	mis	fall/fals
bad; difficult	bad	wrong	wrong; bad	false

Roots Volume 1

Lesson 12: Hear, See, Feel

audi	spect	vis	sens/sent	tact/tang
hear	see; look	see	feel	feel; touch

circumspect   envisage   dissent   audible   tactile
visionary   sentient   auditory   spectacle   tangible

Step 1: Examine the Words
How well do you know them? What can you tell about them?

New Words	Familiar Words	Known Words	Mastered Words
words I do not know; unfamiliar words	words I recognize but cannot fully define	words I understand but don't use often	words I know well and use regularly

1. **Sentient** is what form of *sentience*? _____

2. Many familiar words include the roots **vis**, **audi**, and **spect**. List as many additional words as you can think of that include these roots.

AUDI   VIS   SPECT

101

Roots Volume 1 — Lesson 12

> **STEP 2: Figure Out Meaning**
> Using context and your knowledge of roots, write the <u>sentence number</u> of the bolded word next to the best definition below. *Note: Not all definitions will be used.*

1. Can you **envisage** how the house will look once when finish the renovations?

2. With nine of the ten team members concurring, Emily was the only one to **dissent**.

3. Tressa was a **visionary** school principal who started a computer program at her school years before most schools realized the importance of technology education.

4. Pigs are **sentient** animals that can experience happiness, fear, and sorrow.

5. Because the music was barely **audible**, we asked him to turn up the volume.

6. Helen was diagnosed with an **auditory** disorder after failing three hearing tests.

7. Amy loved **tactile** activities like squishing clay and running her fingers through sand.

8. The circus was a brilliant **spectacle** of lights, costumes, and dizzying acrobatics.

9. Your theory makes sense, but without **tangible** evidence such as fingerprints, you will be unable to prove your case.

10. Paul was **circumspect** in his business dealings and double-checked everything.

to be unable to see or visualize	to visualize; to see in one's mind	able to feel (mentally or emotionally)	related to hearing	able to be heard	able to imagine what will be important in the future
something interesting or exciting to see	relating to the sense of touch	impossible to experience through the five senses	careful or cautious; suspicious	to disagree with a prevailing opinion or decision	physically real; able to be physically touched

Roots Volume 1 — Lesson 12

> **STEP 3: Use Words in Sentences**
> For each sentence on the next page, fill in the word from the list that <u>best</u> fits the blank. *Note: Words may be used twice.*

Root	Word	Definition
AUDI — hear	**auditory** (adj)	related to **hearing**
	audible (adj) / *audibility* (n)	able to be **heard**
SPECT — see, look	**spectacle** (n)	a performance or display that is visually remarkable or exciting to **see**
	circumspect (adj)	cautious and careful; suspicious; "**looking** around" to make sure things are okay
VIS — see	**envisage** (v)	to visualize (**see** in one's mind); to predict or anticipate
	visionary (adj) / *visionary* (n)	able to imagine what the future will or should look like; able to "**see**" the future with wisdom
SENS, SENT — feel	**sentient** (adj) / *sentience* (n)	able to mentally or emotionally **feel**
	dissent (v) / *dissention* (n)	to openly disagree with a prevailing opinion or decision; to "not **feel**" the same as others
TACT, TANG — feel, touch	**tactile** (adj)	related to the sense of physical **touch**
	tangible (adj) / *tangibility* (n)	physically real (not existing only in one's mind); able to be **felt** through physical touch

103

Roots Volume 1 — Lesson 12

1. Focused only on the present and giving hardly a thought to the future, Marc was certainly not a(n) _____ leader.

2. To ensure that his speech would be _____ to all in the room, Evan had an expensive new sound system installed.

3. Kate had a rare _____ disorder and could not feel the difference between velvet and wool.

4. Lucy wore the gold locket as a(n) _____ reminder of her late grandmother.

5. Close your eyes and _____ a world of peace and harmony.

6. It is wise to be _____ when being offered a deal that seems too good to be true.

7. Andy wondered whether _____ and intelligent beings existed in outer space.

8. Always _____, Julia continually looked over her shoulder as they walked down the path.

9. The international dance show was a true _____ that brought the audience to its feet in thunderous applause.

10. Certain sounds that are _____ to cats and dogs cannot be detected by humans.

11. When learning a foreign language, it is important to get a lot of _____ practice in addition to practice speaking and writing.

12. Asked whether she found the new rules to be fair, Chloe _____ and said they were completely unjust.

13. Prince Gerald could _____ the chaos that would ensue if he abandoned the throne, but he fled in the night nevertheless.

14. Her teddy bear was nice, but Anna wanted a(n) _____ pet that could truly love her back.

Roots Volume 1

Lesson 12

> **STEP 4: Mixed Review**
> How much do you remember? Let's find out!

1. A society in which nearly all citizens are **oppressed** could be classified as:
   - a. empathetic
   - b. uncouth
   - c. a dystopia
   - d. altruistic

2. Something **fall**acious is:
   - a. untrue
   - b. bad
   - c. evil
   - d. correct

3. *Phon* means "sound." Something **euphonious**:
   - a. sounds bad
   - b. cannot be heard
   - c. makes no sound
   - d. sounds good

4. If something is **heterogeneous**, it is made up of _____ people or elements.
   - a. good
   - b. different
   - c. similar
   - d. many

5. Which might you use to cure a **malady** caused by a poison?
   - a. a pandemic
   - b. an antidote
   - c. a colleague
   - d. an obstruction

6. Most European languages, including English, are part of the _____ language family.
   - a. Indo-European
   - b. Germanic
   - c. Romance
   - d. Latin

7. **Benevolent** and **malevolent** are:
   - a. synonyms
   - b. homophones
   - c. antonyms
   - d. unrelated

8. *Transient* is to *permanent* as **extrovert** is to:
   - a. introvert
   - b. extricate
   - c. subvert
   - d. exodus

9. If you have a **surplus** of something, you have:
   - a. many different kinds
   - b. all of it
   - c. more than enough
   - d. none of it

10. **Fallacy** and **bonanza** are:
    - a. synonyms
    - b. homophones
    - c. antonyms
    - d. unrelated

Roots Volume 1 — Lesson 12

11. *Four plus four equals ten* is an example of a(n) _____ statement.
    a. erroneous
    b. hypocritical
    c. eccentric
    d. symbiotic

12. Lou's parents were distressed by his **errant** behavior.
    a. dangerous
    b. unusual
    c. cruel
    d. wrong

13. If two things are of the same value or function, you might say they are:
    a. symbiotic
    b. equitable
    c. homogeneous
    d. equivalent

14. The **synthesis** of two things is when they come together to:
    a. make something good
    b. make something new
    c. make something bad
    d. none of the above

15. After a week of *thinking carefully about his feelings and hopes*, Marvin decided he wanted to become a doctor and applied to medical school.
    a. extrication
    b. introspection
    c. deducing
    d. immersion

16. If you are experiencing **seclusion**, you are experiencing:
    a. not having things you need
    b. being oppressed by an authority
    c. unfair judgment
    d. being away from others

17. If people are lavishing you with **effusive** praise, they are giving praise that:
    a. gushes out enthusiastically
    b. is implied but not spoken
    c. is insincere
    d. is kind and helpful

18. Something _____ is unclear because it can have more than one interpretation.
    a. posthumous
    b. ambiguous
    c. incoherent
    d. omnipotent

19. Which has the OPPOSITE meaning to **obstruct**?
    a. to block
    b. to give power to
    c. to let pass through
    d. to go through

20. Rebecca vowed to *get back at* whomever had ruined her painting.
    a. prevail over
    b. antagonize
    c. segregate
    d. retaliate against

Roots Volume 1

Lesson 12

STEP 5: Write the Words
Write each word one more time (in any order). Be sure to spell correctly!

> circumspect envisage dissent audible tactile
> visionary sentient auditory spectacle tangible

_____   _____

_____   _____

_____   _____

_____   _____

_____   _____

STEP 6: Dig a Little Deeper
Deepen and express your understanding in different ways.

Look at the pairs of words below. For each pair, write one sentence that incorporates both words.

visionary + envisage   **audible + spectacle**   **sentient + circumspect**

Sentence 1:

Sentence 2:

Sentence 3:

Roots Volume 1 — Lesson 12

> **STEP 7: Examine Other Words**
> Check any word you already know well.
> Put an **X** next to words you do not know well or do not know at all.

AUDI	SPECT	VIS
☐ auditorium	☐ specter	☐ visual
☐ audiocassette	☐ spectrum	☐ invisible
☐ audience	☐ inspect	☐ visor
☐ audacious	☐ spectator	☐ vision
☐ audacity	☐ spectacles	☐ vista

SENS/SENT	TACT/TANG
☐ sense	☐ tact
☐ sensation	☐ tactical
☐ sensible	☐ tactician
☐ sensory	☐ intangible

> **STEP 8: Reflect on the Meaning of New Words**
> Choose two of the words that you do not already know and look up their meanings. Consider how the **root** in each word may relate to its meaning.

Word:

Meaning:

Word:

Meaning:

audi	spect	vis	sens/sent	tact/tang
hear	see; look	see	feel	feel; touch

Roots Volume 1 — Lesson 13

Lesson 13: One, Two

uni	mono	sol	bi	di/du
one	one	alone	two	two

dichotomy   unify   bilateral   solitude   duplicitous
monotonous   desolate   unanimous   monopoly   bisect

Step 1: Examine the Words
How well do you know them? What can you tell about them?

New Words *words I do not know; unfamiliar words*	Familiar Words *words I recognize but cannot fully define*	Known Words *words I understand but don't use often*	Mastered Words *words I know well and use regularly*

For each word below, circle the suffix and write the suggested part of speech.

1. *desolation* _____

2. *bilaterally* _____

3. *unanimity* _____

4. *unify* _____

5. *monopolize* _____

Roots Volume 1 — Lesson 13

> **STEP 2: Figure Out Meaning**
> Using context and your knowledge of roots, write the <u>sentence number</u> of the bolded word next to the best definition below. *Note: Not all definitions will be used.*

1. The decision will not be **unanimous** unless every one of us votes for it.

2. While some people love crowds and excitement, others prefer **solitude** and quiet.

3. Famine served to **unify** the two warring tribes, as they were forced to hunt together to survive.

4. The class was bored by Mr. Totter's dull, **monotonous** voice.

5. Felipe wrote an essay on the **dichotomy** of good and evil.

6. With only a few remaining open shops, the mall was **desolate** and hauntingly quiet.

7. Please **bisect** the squash before cooking it, and be sure that the two halves are the same size and thickness.

8. The presidents of both countries agreed to hold a **bilateral** peace conference.

9. Britain had a **monopoly** on steel-making for many years, until finally a few other nations began to produce steel as well.

10. Though his words rang true, I could tell he was lying by his sly, **duplicitous** smile.

complete control of something by one group	the state of being alone (often intentionally)	to bring together as one	dull and repetitive; not changing in tone/pitch	to cut in half or in two pieces	to feel one emotion at all times
involving two parties or nations	twice as valuable as important	lonely, sad, or bleak; empty of people	deceitful; sneaky; "two-faced"	strong contrast between two things	agreed to by everyone

Roots Volume 1 — Lesson 13

> **STEP 3: Use Words in Sentences**
> For each sentence on the next page, fill in the word from the list that <u>best</u> fits the blank. *Note: Words may be used twice.*

UNI one	**unify** (v)	to bring different ideas or people together as **one**
	unanimous (adj) *unanimously (adv)*	agreed to by every**one**
MONO one	**monopoly** (n) *monopolize (v)*	complete control or ownership of something by **one** person or group
	monotonous (adj)	dull, boring; repetitive, unchanging; of **one** tone only
SOL alone	**solitude** (n)	the state of being all **alone** (often intentionally)
	desolate (adj) *desolation (n)*	(of a place) **lonely**, sad; empty of people
BI two	**bilateral** (adj) *bilaterally (adv)*	involving or happening between **two** groups or nations
	bisect (v)	to cut in **two** parts (cut in half)
DI/DU two	**dichotomy** (n)	a strong contrast or division between **two** things
	duplicitous (adj) *duplicity (n)*	deceitful; sneaky; "**two**-faced"

Roots Volume 1 — Lesson 13

1. France and Germany engaged in _____ negotiations to develop a new trade deal between the two countries.

2. Though everyone assumed Jennie was telling the truth, I knew her to be _____ and sly.

3. Showing different groups people what they have in common is a good way to begin to _____ them.

4. Tom's voice was so _____ that I couldn't keep my eyes open.

5. Most city council members concurred with the proposal to build a new mall, but because two members dissented, it was not a(n) _____ decision.

6. Fascinated by the _____ of light and dark, Daysia painted a series of landscape murals highlighting the difference between night and day.

7. It was a(n) _____ street, with discarded junk, abandoned houses, and no signs of life or happiness.

8. If you don't _____ the cake evenly, one of the twins will complain that his half is smaller.

9. The Harrison brothers had a(n) _____ on the lumber trade and chased away any other lumber dealers who tried to settle in town.

10. In a(n) _____ ruling, every member of the court upheld the validity of the new law.

11. After a series of successful _____ talks, the leaders of the two nations invited other countries to join in their discussions.

12. Cathy was bored by the _____ chore of stacking papers and begged for more varied and interesting work.

13. I find it easier to be introspective when I am in complete _____, away from the distraction of other people.

14. After the fire, the field was a(n) _____ wasteland where children no longer ran and played.

Roots Volume 1

Lesson 13

> **STEP 4: Mixed Review**
> How much do you remember? Let's find out!

1. Alison had a <u>premonition</u> about the earthquake. That means she had:
    a. a strong fear of it afterwards
    b. the power to stop it
    c. in-depth understanding of it
    d. a feeling beforehand that it would occur

2. Something **dysfunctional**:
    a. doesn't work as it should
    b. is bad or evil
    c. doesn't sound good
    d. is strange and terrifying

3. Which is a reason someone might *falsify* a document?
    a. to check whether it is true
    b. to make it easier to understand
    c. to check whether it is false
    d. to cover up a lie

4. In order to <u>envisage</u> something, you need:
    a. omnipresence
    b. imagination
    c. circumspection
    d. omnipotence

5. The Mighty Memory baseball team wins five games, loses one, then wins seven more. The game they lose is:
    a. an aberration
    b. a fallacy
    c. erroneous
    d. malevolent

6. **Which of the following is most likely to be considered a <u>spectacle</u>?**
    a. peaceful conflict resolution
    b. a muddy pond
    c. a huge fireworks display
    d. doing well on a math quiz

7. Someone who is **heterodox** does not always _____ with authority figures.
    a. subvert
    b. intercede
    c. concur
    d. interject

8. Olivia was **ambivalent** about whether to speak to the **multitude** or keep things to herself.
    a. reticent . . . group
    b. unsure . . . crowd
    c. impartial . . . group
    d. reticent . . . crowd

9. A **superlative hyperbole** would be:
    a. being good at being dishonest
    b. too much exaggeration
    c. a weak or "below-level" statement
    d. an excellent exaggeration

Roots Volume 1

Lesson 13

10. ***Hypocrisy*** and ***misconstrue*** are:
    a. synonyms
    b. homophones
    c. antonyms
    d. unrelated

11. **Audible** is to *hearing* as **tangible** is to:
    a. seeing
    b. touch
    c. emotions
    d. hands

12. To ***dissent*** is to:
    a. disagree
    b. separate
    c. go along with
    d. refuse

13. Which is most likely to be considered a ***misfortune***?
    a. being kind
    b. losing all of your money
    c. misinterpreting a joke
    d. trying hard

14. A SEMIANNUAL EVENT TAKES PLACE:
    A. TWICE A MONTH
    B. EVERY TWO YEARS
    C. EVERY YEAR
    D. EVERY SIX MONTHS

15. Robin Hood's men plotted to **undermine** the sheriff's power in the land.
    a. extricate
    b. subvert
    c. deprive
    d. subpar

16. Which of the following is a ***tactile experience***?
    a. watching a dance performance
    b. listening to beautiful music
    c. squeezing a stress ball
    d. feeling nervous or uneasy

17. If you are ***circumspect*** about something, you:
    a. do not trust it automatically
    b. go around it
    c. have two feelings about it
    d. look around it

18. Jeremiah ***abhorred*** the drawings because they were **not good enough**.
    a. hated . . . hypocritical
    b. hated . . . subpar
    c. threw away . . . hypocritical
    d. threw away . . . subpar

19. If something is very simple, it is not:
    a. hypercritical
    b. segregated
    c. heterogeneous
    d. multifaceted

Roots Volume 1 — Lesson 13

STEP 5: Write the Words
Write each word one more time (in any order). Be sure to spell correctly!

> dichotomy   unify   bilateral   solitude   duplicitous
> monotonous   desolate   unanimous   monopoly   bisect

_____   _____

_____   _____

_____   _____

_____   _____

_____   _____

STEP 6: Dig a Little Deeper
Deepen and express your understanding in different ways.

Look over the roots and words below. Which number is represented by each root?
Write the number in the box provided. (Note: Numbers are not in order.)
Note: If you do not know and cannot deduce an answer, look it up! ☺

TRI triangle, triathlon, triad		HEX hexagon	
OCT octopus, octagon		QUAD/QUAR quadrilateral, quarter	
PENT pentameter, pentagon		DEC decade, decimal, decathlon	
CENT century, centennial, centenarian		MIL millennium, millimeter	

Roots Volume 1 — Lesson 13

STEP 7: Examine Other Words
Check any word you already know well. Put an **X** next to words you do not know well or do not know at all.

UNI	MONO	SOL
☐ universe	☐ monologue	☐ sole
☐ universal	☐ monocle	☐ solo
☐ unicorn	☐ monochrome	☐ solitary
☐ unicycle	☐ monotone	☐ isolation
	☐ monorail	

BI	DI/DU
☐ bicycle	☐ dioxide
☐ binomial	☐ dual
☐ bipartisan	☐ duo
☐ bifocals	☐ duplex

STEP 8: Reflect on the Meaning of New Words
Choose two of the words that you do not already know and look up their meanings. Consider how the **root** in each word may relate to its meaning.

Word: Word:

Meaning: Meaning:

uni	mono	sol	bi	di/du
one	one	alone	two	two

Roots Volume 1 — Lesson 14

Lesson 14: Forces

pel/puls	ject	ten/tain	pend	tract
push	throw	keep; hold	hang	pull

tenacity   pending   interject   detract   retract
dejected   sustain   compel   dependent   repulsive

Step 1: Examine the Words
How well do you know them? What can you tell about them?

New Words	Familiar Words	Known Words	Mastered Words
words I do not know; unfamiliar words	words I recognize but cannot fully define	words I understand but don't use often	words I know well and use regularly

1. **Compul<u>sion</u>** is what form of *compel*? _____

2. **Repul<u>sion</u>** is what form of *repulsive*? _____

3. **Depend<u>ent</u>** is what form of *dependence*? _____

4. **Detrac<u>tion</u>** is what form of *detract*? _____

5. The suffix of **tenacity** suggests what part of speech? _____

6. The suffix of **tenuous** suggests what part of speech? _____

117

Roots Volume 1 — Lesson 14

> **STEP 2: Figure Out Meaning**
> Using context and your knowledge of roots, write the <u>sentence number</u> of the bolded word next to the best definition below. *Note: Not all definitions will be used.*

1. When he heard Mary giving the others erroneous information, he was quick to **interject** and correct her.

2. Because Thalia was usually so accurate and thorough, her small mistake did not **detract** from her excellent reputation.

3. Why do some people find cockroaches **repulsive**? I think they are adorable!

4. Maritza persevered despite every challenge, and we admired her **tenacity**.

5. Only when the monster stepped away and began to **retract** its razor-sharp teeth into its jaw did Margie begin to think she might survive the horrific encounter.

6. The frazzled parents tried desperately to **compel** their son to eat his vegetables.

7. All mammals are **dependent** on adults at birth; none can survive on their own.

8. The Marlins could not earn enough money to **sustain** their extravagant lifestyle, so they had to sell their cars and move to a smaller home.

9. After losing the ball game, Santiago felt frustrated and **dejected**.

10. We cannot comment on the case while the investigation is still **pending**, but after the case is closed we will explain everything to the public.

awful; horrid; disgusting	to leave or go away suddenly	the ability to hold on and not give up	to hold on to negative thoughts or feelings	to keep (something) going; to hold up	to push (someone) to do something
to take away from; to lessen or reduce	relying on someone or something else	unresolved; awaiting a conclusion; in process	to interrupt by throwing in a comment	to pull back or take back	sad or depressed; emotionally down

Roots Volume 1 — Lesson 14

> **STEP 3: Use Words in Sentences**
> For each sentence on the next page, fill in the word from the list that <u>best</u> fits the blank. *Note: Words may be used twice.*

Root	Word	Definition
PEL/PULS push	**compel** (v) *compelling (adj)*	to **push** (someone) to do something
	repulsive (adj) *repulsion (n)*	so horrid or awful that it "**pushes**" you away; disgusting
JECT throw	**dejected** (adj) *dejection (n)*	sad or depressed; emotionally "**thrown** down"
	interject (v) *interjection (n)*	to interrupt; to "**throw** in" a comment in the middle of someone else speaking
TEN/TAIN keep; hold	**tenacity** (n) *tenacious (adj)*	the ability to **hold** on and not give up
	sustain (v) *sustenance (n)*	to **keep** (something) going; to **hold** (something) up; to endure (something unpleasant)
PEND hang	**dependent** (adj) *dependent (n)* *dependence (n)*	relying on something/someone else in order to happen or to function properly; not able to care for oneself; "**hanging**" on another for support
	pending (adj)	still "**hanging**" or unresolved; in process; about to happen
TRACT pull	**detract** (v) *detraction (n)*	to take away from (something); to lessen or **pull** down (status or reputation); to distract from
	retract (v) *retraction (n)* *retractable (adj)*	to **pull** or take (something) back; to withdraw (a statement)

Roots Volume 1 — Lesson 14

1. Orson was forced to _____ his statement when the facts could not be verified.

2. Mr. Bakshi looked forward to his daughter's _____ wedding.

3. The silver statue was so stunning that even a few scratches and dents did not _____ from its beauty.

4. Feeling _____, Hal hung his head and let a tear slide down his cheek.

5. What on earth would _____ someone to put sour cream on a peanut butter sandwich?

6. The toy robot could _____ its arms and legs and become a ship.

7. The teacher's decision to cancel the field trip left the children feeling _____.

8. Gia thought a lot about what might _____ people to be more altruistic and benevolent.

9. Always a reticent man, Nolan wanted desperately to join in the conversation but was afraid to _____.

10. After months of perseverance, Nora's _____ failed her; she finally abandoned her quest.

11. Philip tried to enjoy working with the rodents at the pet store, but he found them so _____ he finally had to ask someone else to do it.

12. The old stone wall was not strong enough to _____ the weight of all the people.

13. Two weeks after the contest officially ended, the results were still _____ and a winner had not yet been declared.

14. The Smiths were _____ on each other and never liked to be apart.

Roots Volume 1

Lesson 14

> **Step 4: Mixed Review**
> How much do you remember? Let's find out!

1. **Omnipresence** *is the state of:*
    a. knowing all
    b. being everywhere at once
    c. being all-powerful
    d. being generous and kind

2. You cannot experience **dejection** if you are not:
    a. compatible
    b. benevolent
    c. duplicitous
    d. sentient

3. If a decision is **unanimous**, then there is no one who:
    a. falsifies
    b. misconstrues
    c. dissents
    d. concurs

4. If you **persevere**, then you demonstrate:
    a. tenacity
    b. altruism
    c. solitude
    d. dichotomy

5. If something is **monotonous**, you might find it:
    a. frightening
    b. dull and boring
    c. in only one place
    d. at only one time

6. Una wrote a poem on the **great difference between** love and hatred.
    a. dichotomy of
    b. monopoly of
    c. unification of
    d. abhorrence for

7. Which is the best example of **eccentric** behavior?
    a. donating money to charity
    b. speaking quietly
    c. not giving up
    d. wearing only red clothing

8. If you **deduce** something, you figure it out:
    a. easily
    b. afterwards
    c. based on evidence
    d. beforehand

9. The salesman claimed that the liquid was a ____ that would cure every ____.
    a. malady . . . panacea
    b. pandemic . . . malady
    c. panacea . . . malady
    d. pandemic . . . panacea

10. Something **unambiguous** is:
    a. clear
    b. confusing
    c. boring
    d. powerful

Roots Volume 1

Lesson 14

11. Something done with *malice* is done with:
    a. bad intentions
    b. good intentions
    c. no feeling
    d. no manners

12. **Posterity** is an <u>antonym</u> for:
    a. crowds
    b. ancestors
    c. children
    d. solitude

13. ***Duplicitous*** is to *honesty* as ***benevolent*** is to:
    a. misgivings
    b. altruism
    c. good intentions
    d. bad intentions

14. THE *SYNTHESIS* OF TWO THINGS IS WHEN THEY COME TOGETHER TO:
    A. MAKE SOMETHING GOOD
    B. MAKE SOMETHING NEW
    C. MAKE SOMETHING BAD
    D. NONE OF THE ABOVE

15. Which pair of words are *antonyms*?
    a. euphoria . . . apathy
    b. bona fide . . . verify
    c. monopoly . . . omnipotence
    d. unify . . . segregate

16. Which of the following is *audible*?
    a. sunshine
    b. clapping
    c. a hand wave
    d. soft velvet

17. Living in a *desolate* environment might make someone feel:
    a. dejected
    b. unanimous
    c. tangible
    d. equitable

18. *Someone who can imagine the future with wisdom might be called a(n):*
    a. spectacle
    b. dystopia
    c. visionary
    d. aberration

19. If you prove the *veracity* of something, you prove that it is:
    a. false
    b. true
    c. fake
    d. good

20. *I canceled the event because I had serious _____ whether we could sell enough tickets.*
    a. misgivings about
    b. empathy toward
    c. impartiality for
    d. euphemisms for

Roots Volume 1 — Lesson 14

STEP 5: Write the Words
Write each word one more time (in any order). Be sure to spell correctly!

> tenacity   pending   interject   detract   retract
> dejected   sustain   compel   dependent   repulsive

_____   _____
_____   _____
_____   _____
_____   _____
_____   _____

STEP 6: Dig a Little Deeper
Deepen and express your understanding in different ways.

Throughout *Roots*, you have seen that many **words are like puzzles** waiting to be pieced together, and roots and prefixes are the pieces you need. Look below at a few more examples, combining **pel** and four of the prefixes you have learned:

compel → com + pel = "with push"   **repel** → re + pel = "push back"
dispel → dis + pel = "push away"   **propel** → pro + pel = "push forth"

See how you can make sense of these words? There are thousands of words like this in our language – words that can be broken into parts and deciphered when you know the most common roots and prefixes. So remember:

*Whenever you encounter new words in your reading,
look for parts you recognize. You may be surprised how much
you can figure out based just on what you have learned in this book!*

Roots Volume 1 — Lesson 14

> **STEP 7: Examine Other Words**
> Check any word you already know well.
> Put an **X** next to words you do not know well or do not know at all.

PEL/PULS	JECT	TEN/TAIN
☐ impel	☐ trajectory	☐ detention
☐ expel	☐ reject	☐ tenuous
☐ compel	☐ project	☐ tentative
☐ propel		☐ retain
☐ pulse		☐ maintain
☐ impulse		☐ sustain
☐ compulsion		☐ abstain

PEND	TRACT
☐ pendulum	☐ contract
☐ depend	☐ traction
☐ suspend	☐ protracted
☐ pendant	

> **STEP 8: Reflect on the Meaning of New Words**
> Choose two of the words that you do not already know and look up their meanings. Consider how the **root** in each word may relate to its meaning.

Word:

Meaning:

Word:

Meaning:

pel/puls	ject	ten/tain	pend	tract
push	throw	keep; hold	hang	pull

Notes

A full answer key is available at *rootsvocab.com.*

Made in the USA
San Bernardino, CA
03 September 2018